END

I will honestly say that this is one of the finest, most anointed books that I have read in ages. *Seeing with Fresh Eyes* takes me back to my early readings of authors like Andrew Murray and Watchman Nee. Back then, I read as a simple man desiring to find the deep truths of the Word of God. Now, in the same way, my study of John's book has brought me into a more complete understanding of the true gospel of our Lord.

John committed himself to find God's answers to perplexing questions he had about *how* he had been saved and *what* he had been saved from. The more truth he uncovered, the more amazing God became to him. Through his openness, I believe you will find your own victory. *Seeing with Fresh Eyes* will clear up much misunderstanding and ignite a new hunger in you to know the Person of the Holy Spirit. *Seeing with Fresh Eyes* brings Spirit-filled revelation that will change your life and help others as well. Enjoy!

—Dr. Dan Funkhouser
Senior Pastor, Heartbeat Ministries International
International Speaker
Adjunct Instructor, Charis Bible College

Over my fifty years of ministry, this is the best explanation that I have read of the inner workings of salvation, both from God's perspective and our own. *Seeing with Fresh Eyes* will find its place as one of the most relevant books of our generation. Your journey of faith will come alive as you explore the divine narrative and discover how the Bible reveals God's plans for you today.

Reading this book by John Bullock is like getting together with an old friend. You will be encouraged and enriched. You will definitely not be disappointed! This is more than a good read; it is a road map to an awesome life.

—Chaplain (Lieutenant Colonel) W. T. Permenter, USA, Retired

Seeing with Fresh Eyes is more than just a book title—it's a way of life.

I've had the privilege of knowing the author—John Bullock—for a number of years, and if there is one thing that I would say is unique about John, it is that he has a way of seeing beyond what most people notice. In this short study, John has harnessed this talent and focused it on the eternal plan of God for His people. The result is a departure from the clichés and pat answers that we so often repeat without ever having thought them through or even really considering the logic (and more often than not, the lack thereof) behind those answers. The end product of this is a refreshing and often challenging journey of reexamination and discovery.

—Dr. Delron Shirley
International Missionary and Teacher
Founder, Teach All Nations Mission
Former Dean, World Harvest Bible College
and Indiana Christian University

Seeing with Fresh Eyes: Sin, Salvation, and the Steadfast Love of God is not a light read. Be prepared to experience a thought-provoking, insightful, heart-stirring reflection through one person's continuing journey into the depths of a genuine, personal relationship with our Creator God. But I make one promise: If you'll walk through this testimony deliberately, patiently, and with an open heart, you will emerge a different person with a deeper encounter with the living God. You will never regret it, and you will ask for more!

There is a remarkable quote from Beauchene: "You are never a great man when you have more mind than heart." I can confidently tell you three things about John: he is a man of genuine faith in the God of the Scriptures, and he is a man who thinks his way well through that faith—but he is also a man whose values are rooted in his heart. To him, these are not dry facts, especially now that he has dared to risk all, ask those hard questions, and take the necessary but exciting journey that leads ever deeper into growing intimacy with the One who is healing, freedom, and full life.

—David Vandenbergh
Pastoral Care for International Christian Workers,
Barnabas International
Pastor, Christian and Missionary Alliance

Seeing with Fresh Eyes is a fascinating journey from creation to Jesus's resurrection, detailing how God's persevering, unconditional love is more than enough to heal mankind's blindness and brokenness from sin. Few people see the beauty of *how* God skillfully and supernaturally crafted their redemption. John clears away questions about the mess we were in because of sin, why Jesus had to come, and how He accomplished His mission—to bridge the gap between us and Father God. John's book doesn't come from a theoretical understanding of who God is, but from a tangible encounter and revelation—knowing that he is now a son in the kingdom of the Highest. Reading this book will provide you great biblical insight, but greater still, it will open your eyes to see the eternal loving Father who has loved you from the beginning of time.

—Bryan Nutman
Founder and President,
Roots and Wings Ministries International
Director, Ministry Relations,
Andrew Wommack Ministries

SEEING
WITH
FRESH EYES

SEEING WITH FRESH EYES

SIN, SALVATION, AND THE STEADFAST LOVE OF GOD

JOHN W. BULLOCK

FULLY REVISED AND EXPANDED

REDEMPTION PRESS

Published by Redemption Press, PO Box 427, Enumclaw, WA 98022.

Toll-Free (844) 2REDEEM (273-3336)

Redemption Press is honored to present this title in partnership with the author. The views expressed or implied in this work are those of the author. Redemption Press provides our imprint seal representing design excellence, creative content, and high-quality production.

ISBN: 978-1-64645-213-2 (Paperback)
978-1-64645-214-9 (ePub)
978-1-64645-215-6 (Mobi)

Library of Congress Catalog Card Number: 2020916339

CONTENTS

FOREWORD

After returning from a trip to Israel, I made an exhibit in my office of several antiquities that I had collected—displayed on an antique table that I had inherited from my grandfather. When my father visited me, I eagerly took him into the room with the announcement, "There's something that I want you to see." Seemingly oblivious to the historical artifacts that dated to the time of Jesus, he responded immediately, "Daddy's table!" Of course, I totally understood that my father was more conditioned to see the family heirloom rather than the two-thousand-year-old relics, but I did walk away from that experience with a clearer perspective on the difference between seeing and looking.

Seeing is a lot harder than looking. We all look at things every day but fail to actually see them. The truth is that we generally only see what we want to see or what we have been trained to see. All we need to do is remember the last disagreement that we had with someone. Both parties were observing the same situation but were seeing it from totally different points of view—like the old analogy of the half-full versus the half-empty glass. The optimist sees the glass as half full because that's the way he wants to see it. The pessimist sees it as half empty because he wants to see it that way. Our training has an equally profound impact on what we see as our perspective. For instance, a seamstress may not be able to admire the beauty of a lovely evening gown simply because her attention is drawn to one simple flaw in the way the dress was sewn together—the old "I can't see the forest for the trees" effect.

Even in spiritual matters, we often speak of seeing things through colored glasses—the filters that we have developed through not only our theological backgrounds, but also our general life experiences. I remember one student in my class at seminary who loved to approach the professor after every class with a comment about his takeaway from the class. Unfortunately, his comment was always the same no matter what the topic of the discussion had been that day: "Sir, it all boils down to 'let your light shine before men so that they can see your good works and glorify your Father which is in heaven.'" I never figured out how he could come to that conclusion after a class on the theory of the pretribulation rapture, the six-day creation, or the Old Testament prophecies of the crucifixion of Jesus, but he had somehow been so powerfully impacted by that principle that it seemed to be the only thing that he could see in any biblical passage or discussion.

Seeing with Fresh Eyes is a compelling invitation for us to put aside our colored glasses—our opinionated viewpoints and our programmed responses—so that we can take a new, unbiased look at the plans and purposes of God for our lives. In this little volume, John Bullock has done something that he has a habit of doing in every area of life—seeing rather than simply looking. Seeing the heart of God in the Scriptures rather than just looking at what we want to find or what we have been trained to find. Each page is an "eye opener" and a whole lot more; it is an invitation to a whole new life of *seeing* rather than just looking.

Dr. Delron Shirley
International Missionary and Teacher
Founder, Teach All Nations Mission

I believe that to him who obeys, and thus opens the doors of his heart to receive the eternal gift, God gives the spirit of his son, the spirit of himself, to be in him, and lead him to the understanding of all truth; that the true disciple shall thus always know what he ought to do, though not necessarily what another ought to do; that the spirit of the father and the son enlightens by teaching righteousness.

I believe that no teacher should strive to make men think as he thinks, but to lead them to the living Truth, to the Master himself, of whom alone they can learn anything, who will make them in themselves know what is true by the very seeing of it. I believe that the inspiration of the Almighty alone gives understanding. I believe that to be the disciple of Christ is the end of being; that to persuade men to be his disciples is the end of teaching.

—George MacDonald,
"Justice" in *Unspoken Sermons*

INTRODUCTION

My Awakening

*Stand in the ways and see, and ask for the old
paths, where the good way is, and walk in it;
then you will find rest for your souls.*
Jeremiah 6:16

Some time ago I realized that although I had grown
up in a Bible-believing church, I didn't really understand the gospel. Oh, I certainly knew facts about the
gospel. I knew I was a sinner and was condemned to die
because of my sins and unrighteousness. I knew God had
sent His Son, Jesus, as a man, so that through His death
and resurrection I could be freed from that condemnation.
I knew that, once freed, I would also have the power to live
a victorious life.

I knew the facts, but somewhere deep down I knew I
had missed the heart of the message, of the miracle. I knew
the gospel message I was supposed to share with others,
but I still didn't understand the passion and motivation
that had moved Jesus's disciples to leave all and risk everything to reach the nations. Their motivation wasn't only
from a new philosophy or a duty. Something within them
had changed radically. They seemed to laugh at the idea of
self-preservation and gladly traded that for the opportu-

nity to share the gospel. What was that message? Whatever it was, it was transformational. I saw rules and morality around me, but very few transformations.

At one point, I went to one of the gentlemen in our congregation who obviously and unashamedly loved Jesus. The church wasn't sedate, but this man still stood out. He constantly talked about Jesus, but his witness, unlike that of others, didn't seem to come from duty, but instead came from an unabashed overflow of love. I wanted to know why. When I asked him what made the difference, he looked at me, bewildered at my question, and blurted out, "But it's Jesus!" That didn't help me at all. I knew what he said was true, but I was hoping to find something I didn't already suspect—something safe, like a better rationale for my understanding. In hindsight, my question was misguided. I didn't need more knowledge *about* God; I needed more relationship *with* God.

I determined to read the Gospels with an open mind. Instead of presuming to know what they were saying based on prior teaching or my presuppositions, I let them speak to me and say what they would. I determined that if I came to a puzzling text, *I* was the one confused, not the text. Focusing on the authors' continuity of context and concepts opened my eyes. My preconceptions and prejudices, my tendency to think, *Oh, I already know all about this section, so I'll read it quickly*, blinded me to real gems of truth. This book includes many Scripture quotations. Don't rush through them, but thoughtfully consider them.

This book tells of my journey through my questions and discoveries. It is neither comprehensive nor exhaustive, so I'm trusting it will stimulate my readers to study further on their own. You will find treasures because God loves questions; they are His opportunities to teach. The more questions I asked and the more I searched, the more amazing and wonderful God became to me. His love for us is fierce, and His path of salvation is clear—and better than I knew. Far from finessing around with legal loopholes of mercy versus justice, Jesus came to destroy sin, death, and all the resultant works of the devil. He is the healer and restorer. God is love, mercy, justice, and righteousness, with no compromise between them.

Others also have questions. Throughout Christendom, I see individuals reexamining their long-held beliefs. These people admit they became disillusioned with the Christianity they had been taught, but still learned enough of God to say, like Peter, "Lord, to whom shall we go? You have the words of eternal life" (John 6:68). There is truth to be had, but it is out of focus, and therefore is frustratingly out of reach.

However, my discovery process wasn't born of either disillusionment or skepticism. It was born of belief. I knew that at the center of whatever experiences I encountered—joyful or painful—God was unwaveringly good. But I didn't always understand *good*, and that was frustrating. There were gaps in my understanding. I needed to dig in and ask more *how* than *why* questions. It was much like taking apart a fine watch, already knowing its purpose and value, but marveling at its design and how that purpose was accomplished.

Like the ways of God, there are many moving parts,

but they ultimately work together to precisely accomplish the goal of the designer and the purpose of the watch. The watch is the glory of the designer. The designer receives praise, honor, and respect for the way the watch functions. In the same way, my understanding of the love, complexity, and sacrifice that made my salvation possible brings glory to God in the form of my honor, praise, awe, and love. He gets even more glory when I purposefully live in the knowledge, freedom, and power of the salvation He opened to me. Then others see the results.

Doubts are allowed and questions are good. The true gospel invites examination and stands up under scrutiny. An unexamined and untested belief system is not faith. It's only an inheritance you've been taught. Any quest to find the truth requires a willingness to give up what's found to be not true. Separating from traditions you're invested in is unsettling. Worse is negotiating the minefields of friendships with those who are personally threatened by your questioning. Those who question shouldn't be feared or abandoned by the church. These are the people who become solid in what they believe (James 1:2–5). The work of the church is not to combat those who question; it's to proclaim and explain the gospel of Jesus the Christ.

For those thirsting after God, the good questions never end. The danger for all of us is slipping into the belief that life is static and that once you find the right set of facts— "the truth"—everything is settled. The truth is that the Truth is the Person who was and is and is to come.

Jesus has no problem with our questions, our deconstructions, or our efforts to know the truth and live in it. He was most critical of the self-righteous—those who prided themselves on having all the answers and looking down on those who didn't. At the end, His call to us is to Himself, and nowhere else.

As a fellow truth seeker, I welcome you.

CHAPTER 1

Finding the Right Story

If you can't explain it simply,
then you don't understand it.
—Dad

KEY: The Genesis story isn't about the mechanics of creation; it's about the dynamics of relationship.

I discovered during my years as a Christian that there are certain "Questions That Shall Not Be Asked." It's not that they shouldn't be asked, but asking them was embarrassing. For example, a subject like salvation should be basic knowledge, I thought. If I didn't understand it all, then that meant I was deficient and still immature in the faith, right? What was I doing trying to teach others? Another was, "I know God loves me, but I'm not feeling real love back to Him. What's the matter with me?" I remember wishing there had been a book of those shall-not-be-asked answers so I could settle matters with minimal personal upset, benefiting from someone else's wrestling, not mine. But that isn't possible.

I began to notice that those same questions were also causing discomfort in others as inconsistencies and gaps in thinking were exposed. Questions can be threatening to our settled order of understanding; they tend to peek around the corner at us just as we start to feel secure in our analysis of things. I also noticed that people tended to divide into two groups: those who wanted truth above all and were willing to search for themselves—giving up what they found to be untrue to welcome the truth—and a second group, heavily dependent on respected people to tell them what was true and how to believe. This second group could get quite annoyed at persistent questions, even angry.

Here's my confession: I became a Christian at a very early age and grew up trusting the doctrine I had been taught. I knew it was my duty to share the good news of the gospel with others—comfortably and unashamedly. However, as I grew into my teens, when it came to talking about the cross, it just got awkward. I knew I was to spread the good news of freedom in and through Christ, but I stumbled trying to explain this need for human sacrifice in our modern culture. No matter how I told the story, at the core of this "good news" was the cross.

The whole process had been explained to me in many ways, and on some level, I understood. I knew there had to be some connection to the animal sacrifices in the Old Testament, but I didn't understand why our redemption had to be done that way. I understood the models that attempted to explain it—ransom, substitution, etc.—but I still knew there was something I wasn't seeing.

I had no problem believing that Jesus was God, that He had become incarnate, and that somehow, mysteriously, He had died for my sins and rose again. I just didn't understand how—how the cross, how His blood, and how

His resurrection reconciled me back to God. Startlingly, I soon found that others weren't sure either. Worse, just like me, they had also been taught that it was "a mystery that we can't be expected to fully understand." But how could I fully trust what I was unable to understand? God had promised that we did not need to be ignorant. In fact, He took extra care to make sure that those who followed Him were *not* ignorant (Luke 8:10; John 16:13; 1 John 2:20–21). For years I kept these questions to myself and called it faith.

And that worked. On one hand, it didn't hamper my relationship with Jesus or my growing in faith and knowledge, but on the other hand, it did hold me back from evangelism. When explaining the gospel to someone who had never heard it, I almost always felt apologetic—like I had to qualify what I was saying. "I know this sounds strange but . . ." Even though this was the good news through which we are set free, and therefore I should be sharing it confidently and eagerly, what lay behind the story, for me, seemed somehow suspect and disturbingly disconnected.

I knew that in order to arrive at the solution, I first had to understand the problem. If I had trouble understanding the *how* and *why* of my salvation, it was very likely because I didn't understand my dilemma. I also suspected I wasn't seeing God's perspective of things. If the entirety of the Bible was a redemption story of how God moved to restore what humankind, through Adam, had lost in Eden, then I needed to understand what had been lost and how. I started reading the Gospels, but I quickly realized that the book of Genesis was where I needed to start.

As I studied, I realized that—although I had been taught that the message of Genesis was a general chronology from God's creation of the world through the birth of Israel as God's chosen people—producing a detailed history did not seem to be the primary goal of the author. The timelines and history were only his means to an end—to tell an even grander story of God's goodness and love for all of mankind.

For example, the difference between Genesis chapters 1 and 2 had always been a puzzle to me. It's almost like, after telling all about the creation of the heavens and the earth, the author starts over again in chapter 2 to retell the story, this time focusing on Adam—his creation, location, and job responsibilities. Why this do-over? Why didn't he just tell the whole story in one telling?

It was only after I gave up my need to sort out the chronology that I began to see the picture the author was painting. The first chapter is about God Almighty creating the heavens and the earth, but we don't see why He did it. He was LORD, and there was no need to explain. However, in the second chapter, God becomes more personal. He interacts with Adam and instructs him in how to live in harmony with both God and the environment that God has created for him. Unlike all the other created creatures, this man is given a personal name: Adam.

In the first chapter we see God as all-powerful creator. In the second, He is God personal and relatable. He orients Adam to his life in the garden. The author of Genesis is showing us two sides of God that inform us about everything to come in the rest of the book—and in the rest of the Bible. He presents God first of all as Lord of all, the highest king and judge. Yet in the second telling, we see God in a priestly role, relating to Adam directly and teaching him the ways of God. Jesus later came in both those roles combined: as a sacral king[1] and as the champion of our redemption (Matt. 21:5; Heb. 4:14–16).

I believe now that Genesis tells us everything we need to know at the beginning of a very long story. For many years I had felt that the creation story was lacking. It left me with questions, and I wanted more details—especially about those "days." Now I realize I had been lured into the wrong story. The story wasn't about the mechanics of creation; it was about the dynamics of relationship. Jesus was there at the beginning, in the creation and through Adam and Eve's temptation, betrayal, and fall. It was also He, with His Father, who set the course for our redemption, deliverance, and restoration (John 1:1–5).

Answers became clearer to me as I saw that Genesis—and really the whole Bible—is more than just a narrative or rule book. It tells its story through pictures and genealogies—vignettes of many lives and many generations—as well as commentary and direction. The goal is always to illuminate the true nature of God, as well as to contrast the natures of mankind when in harmony versus out of harmony with God. They are recorded as object lessons for us to learn from, count the cost, and make our own choices (Josh. 24:14–15; 1 Cor. 10:6–11).

CHAPTER 2

The End Starts in the Beginning

For the word of the LORD is right,
And all His work is done in truth.
He loves righteousness and justice;
The earth is full of the goodness of the LORD.
Psalm 33:4–5

KEY: Adam and Eve usurp the right of law and sentence themselves.

In the beginning God created the heavens and the earth. How did He do it? I don't know. That's part of the mystery, but I believe God has given us everything we need to know about the things that are essential.

On the sixth day, God created man in His own image and according to His likeness:

> Then God said, "Let Us make man in Our image, according to Our likeness; let them have dominion over the fish of the sea, over the birds of the air, and over the cattle, over all the earth and over every creeping thing that creeps on the earth." So God created man in His own image; in the image of God He created him; male and female He created them. Then God blessed

> them, and God said to them, "Be fruitful and
> multiply; fill the earth and subdue it; have do-
> minion over the fish of the sea, over the birds of
> the air, and over every living thing that moves
> on the earth."
>
> . . . Then God saw everything that He had
> made, and indeed it was very good. So the eve-
> ning and the morning were the sixth day. (Gen.
> 1:26–28, 31)

Unlike the first five days of creation, which were declared "good," God described His work on day six, when
He created man, as "very good." Genesis chapter 2 goes
into more detail. Like the animals, man came from the
earth (Gen. 1:24), but unlike the animals, God breathed
the "breath of life" into his nostrils and "man became a living soul." This description was never applied to an animal.

God planted a garden in the land east of Eden (which
means *delight*). He created it especially for the man He had
formed. He planted trees for beauty and for food. We don't
know how large the garden was, but it was a safe place, set
apart from the rest of the world—almost like a modern
gated community. Everything the man needed was there.
A river flowed out of Eden, watering the garden just before
it broke into four new rivers. All the trees were pleasant
to look at and good for food, but two of the trees in the
garden were special: the Tree of Life in the middle of the
garden and the Tree of the Knowledge of Good and Evil.
God put the man in the garden to cultivate it and protect
it (Gen. 2:15). The man did not own it; he was a steward.
The man was the first gardener.

The man could freely eat from any tree in God's garden, but as the owner, God had one restriction: "Of the tree of the knowledge of good and evil you shall not eat, for in the day that you eat of it you shall surely die" (Gen. 2:17). Notice this was not a curse, and the tree was not bait to entrap mankind. God's directive was a warning motivated by love, not manipulation. We are surrounded by similar notices every day: "Beware of Dog," "High Voltage," or "Poison!" All are meant for our protection from things that in the correct environment or application are beneficial, but outside of that may be deadly.

The Tree of the Knowledge of Good and Evil was among the trees listed that were "pleasant to the sight and good for food" (Gen. 2:9). But how could that be true since the man was just told he would die if he ate of it? It appears that any beast in the garden that ate from that tree would find it to be good food. Only Adam was restricted, but Adam had been given a different kind of life than the beasts.

Why was the tree even there? If the garden was made for man, why put a deadly tree in the middle of it? When God gave the man free rein of the entire garden but reserved one tree for Himself, the effect was to remind him that all the good in his life was a gift and that there was a caring Giver behind it all. The tree was not meant to be a snare for man, but a blessing. It was a guard against pride and self-sufficiency. It was originally a reminder of God's goodness and beneficence, but the serpent later twisted it into a symbol of God's domineering withholding from them. Only then did it become a temptation.

God Creates Woman

We'll talk about the temptation later, but here the narrative of the story suddenly changes. First, God decides it's not good for man to be alone. Second, God decides to fix this deficiency by making a helper suitable for and complementary to him. Third, we discover the man's name is Adam.

> And the LORD God said, "It is not good that man should be alone; I will make him a helper comparable to him." Out of the ground the LORD God formed every beast of the field and every bird of the air, and brought them to Adam to see what he would call them. And whatever Adam called each living creature, that was its name. So Adam gave names to all cattle, to the birds of the air, and to every beast of the field. But for Adam there was not found a helper comparable to him.
>
> And the LORD God caused a deep sleep to fall on Adam, and he slept; and He took one of his ribs, and closed up the flesh in its place. Then the rib which the LORD God had taken from man He made into a woman, and He brought her to the man.
>
> And Adam said: "This is now bone of my bones and flesh of my flesh; she shall be called Woman, because she was taken out of Man."
>
> Therefore a man shall leave his father and mother and be joined to his wife, and they shall become one flesh.

> And they were both naked, the man and
> his wife, and were not ashamed. (Gen. 2:18–
> 25)

God formed every beast of the field and every bird of the air and brought them to Adam, who gave names to all of them. But neither he nor God found any like himself; none were comparable. So God put Adam to sleep, took a rib from him, and made Woman. When Adam woke up, he recognized himself. "My bone! My flesh!" She was "after his kind," his perfect complement for companionship as well as for the work of cultivating and caring for the garden. Because God's breath of life was in Adam, and the woman came out of Adam, she also had that special life from God.

Who Is God?

In the opening verses of the creation account, we met the Creator. His name in Hebrew is *Elohim. Elohim* means "supreme one" or "mighty one." The name carries the idea of dominion and rule, like a king. As creator, God is over and above all He creates. Thus, throughout chapter 1, Elohim did two things on each day of creation. He created through proclamations like "Let there be . . ." Creation happened as He decreed. Then, at the end of each day, He judged that day's work and declared His assessment. In each case, it was found to be good, and at the end of the sixth day when God looked over His creation as a whole, He declared it to be "very good" (Gen. 1:31).

However, in chapter 2, after God rested on the seventh day and after He turned His attention to man, the name referring to God changed. Starting in verse 4, He is no lon-ger referred to as only God; He is now called the Lord God. What happened? God is still Elohim, but now there is a new word before that title: *Lord*. *Lord* is the English trans-lation of the Hebrew YHWH, or *Yahweh*, and is the per-sonal and covenant name of God (see Ex. 3:15). In many English Bibles, *Lord* is written in all capital letters because it is a representation of the personal name of God and is therefore honored. The name Yahweh emphasizes His role as Israel's redeemer and covenant partner. It is personal.

In contrast, when the title *God* is used, it is generally a translation of *Elohim* as a general, impersonal term for God. These are both considered holy words because of who they represent. Even today, out of reverence, most Jewish congregations will replace *Yahweh* with *Adonai* (meaning "the Lord," referring only to God) for their liturgical ser-vices, and another name, *HaShem* (meaning "the Name") for ordinary conversation. For this book, I'll use that title instead of Yahweh.

HaShem is used as a kind of nickname—a way of avoid-ing using God's own name. It acknowledges God's position as creator and ruler, but also points to a different kind of relationship with mankind. For example, my father's name was Philip, but I never called him that. It would have been disrespectful. It would have implied that he was my peer and that we were somehow equal. But I never resented that I couldn't call him that. I didn't need nor want to call him by that name because I already had a better relationship with him. He was my father. We were family. I called him *Dad*—a reflection of both respect and intimacy.

The name HaShem holds that same connotation as the word *parent* or *Dad*: one who loves, provides, and protects. HaShem Elohim was both the creator who provided the garden for Adam and the dad who desired to stroll through creation with him and Eve, enjoying it through their eyes. It was a gift that provided all Adam and Eve would ever need.

The first chapter of Genesis describes God as the creator and judge. The whole narrative is filled with power and wisdom. But in chapter 2, there is no judgment as HaShem Elohim—the Lord God—appears and provides for and teaches Adam. He chose a place and planted a garden, creating almost a world within a world, providing trees for beauty and delicious, nourishing food.

Here's the point: God loved the man and provided everything to nourish their intimate relationship. God, as reflected in the name HaShem Elohim, doesn't relate to man only objectively, as someone to be judged, but He also views man subjectively, as someone to be loved. God as YHWH, as HaShem, is not only the king who created all and is its master, but He is also a parent.

HaShem Elohim—the parent God—told Adam he should not eat of the Tree of the Knowledge of Good and Evil (Gen. 2:16–17). Thus, the message was twofold. First, God spoke as creator and king when He commanded Adam to not eat from the tree, and thus expected him to follow His command: "Obey because I commanded you." But He also spoke as a parent, with the message, "Don't eat from the tree because it's not good for you. It will hurt you. Obey because I love you."

Deceit Enters the Garden

In Genesis chapter 3, we are introduced to another character in the garden. The serpent is described as "more cunning than any beast of the field which the Lord God had made" (Gen. 3:1). We are told specifically that the serpent was a beast of the field.[2] Therefore, the fruit of the Tree of the Knowledge of Good and Evil was not forbidden to it. Perhaps that partially explains why, almost in incredulity, he says to the woman, "Has God indeed said, 'You shall not eat of every tree of the garden'?"

Is that even a temptation? The tree had always been there, and up until now Eve had refrained from eating from it. Its presence appears to have never been a temptation to her before. Furthermore, Eve gives an answer that should have sent any temptation far away. She emphatically says, "Of course we can eat of all the trees in the garden! There's only one tree, in the middle of the garden, that we can't eat from. God told us that if we eat from that one, or even touch it, we would die." That's a strong answer that rebuffs the core of the serpent's question.

The serpent, however, was more cunning and subtle than either Eve or I anticipated. The results were poisonous.

I had always been taught that the key to this interaction was the serpent's question, "Has God indeed said . . . ?" I was told that Eve then suddenly doubted God's word and did what she wanted. However, a closer reading of the text in a larger context shows that the serpent's opening question was only to distract Eve from the real poison. Eve reacted to the word *every*. She defended what God had *said*, but in the flare of her defense, she swallowed the lie of who God *was*.

What do I mean? How did I miss it? How did Eve miss it? Because the language is subtle—just a small change.[3]

The serpent was cunning. When he asked Eve, "Has God indeed said, 'You shall not eat of every tree of the garden'?" he wasn't asking about what God said. He was clouding the picture of who God was. The answer to the serpent's question was so obvious that Eve thought of nothing but the answer: "Of course we can eat of every tree in the garden! It's just one we can't eat from (not all of them) or we'll die."

In this question, the serpent subtly dropped the name HaShem when referring to God. Instead, he said, "Has Elohim indeed said, 'You shall not eat . . . '?" (Gen. 3:1). In other words, has the king, the big powerful boss, really told you not to eat from any of the trees in the garden? It advanced the idea that first, the command was unimaginably excessive, and second, it came from someone who was only concerned with control and power.

When Eve made her defense of what God had truly said, she echoed the serpent's name for God: "Elohim has said, 'You shall not eat it, nor shall you touch it, lest you die'" (Gen. 3:2–3). How ironic! In Eve's rush to defend the truth, and in her zeal to get the facts straight, she lost sight of the father-heart of the God who loved her. She lost sight of the God who gave the command for her benefit, not for His ego. The command had been rooted in love, not in a display of power and domination.

I believe it was out of this unbalanced view of God that

Eve added her extra phrase: "Nor shall you touch it" (Gen. 3:3). She made the command stronger than it had been originally. I believe this added caution comes out of her growing uneasiness in contemplating that the owner of the tree was an all-powerful God who might lack compassion. It's the first sign that the serpent's picture of God as being only an overly domineering and jealous creator, and not a parent, was getting through.

Eve's defenses had been cracked open, and it was only a short step for the serpent to inject her soul with the poison, saying, "You will not surely die. For God knows that in the day you eat of it your eyes will be opened, and you will be like God, knowing good and evil" (Gen. 3:4–5). What was the serpent saying? You won't really die. You'll still be up walking around. Elohim only said that to scare you because He knows if you eat from that tree, you'll be like Him. He won't be the only one with an opinion anymore. You will be able to choose what's right and wrong for you, not only what's right and wrong for Him. You can be like Elohim and eat from *all* the trees in the garden.[4] So she reached out and took the fruit.

Once the serpent separated God the caring father from God Almighty in the mind of Eve, she was vulnerable.

The woman saw the tree in a new light now. She was still cautious, but she "saw that the tree was good for food [it really was], that it was pleasant to the eyes [it was truly that also], and a tree desirable to make one wise [in hindsight, wisdom would have been not eating], she took of its fruit and ate. She also gave to her husband with her, and he ate" (Gen. 3:6). By taking the fruit, she broke her own rule of not even touching the fruit, and by eating it, she gave in to her own desire and broke God's command. God had assigned Adam and the woman to care for the garden. He had given them only one restriction—for their benefit.

Unintended Consequences

The consequences of Adam and Eve's choice changed the course of human history. But first, it changed them. The promise of the tree was real. It gave the man and the woman the knowledge of good and evil. The real question is, What was the effect of having that knowledge?

The knowledge of good and evil changes everything. Knowing good and evil is not trivial and is not controllable. The man and the woman instantly began to apply their newfound discernment. Involuntarily, they became judges. There's nothing else one can do with such knowledge. No longer was judgment a quality determination between good and bad; now discernment became a moral assessment between good and evil. Up until the woman took the fruit, God had made all the judgments. His creation on days one through five was pronounced "good." His creation of man was "very good," but it was "not good" that man was alone. Whatever God declared was the way it was. Now there were new judges in the garden.

However, to their own dismay, the first ones they judged were themselves: "Then the eyes of both of them were opened, and they knew that they were naked; and they sewed fig leaves together and made themselves coverings" (Gen. 3:7). They obviously hadn't been walking around with their physical eyes closed until this time, so therefore this is saying that, somehow, "eyes" that they possessed but hadn't been using were now suddenly opened, enabling them to see what they had never perceived before. They saw that they were naked. They had looked at each other before, and Adam had even remarked about her flesh (Gen. 2:23), but now they were seeing something else: their lack.

Judgment always focuses on lack—on what's been taken or what's been unjustly withheld. Adam and the woman saw their lack of clothing. They knew things were much different now; they could feel it. Their consciences were awakened, and they were ashamed. Although they were still looking at the same bodies that God had called very good, something ominous had changed inside. They no longer saw the world or themselves through God's eyes. The serpent was right when he said, "In the day you eat of it your eyes will be opened, and you will be like God, knowing good and evil" (Gen. 3:5). Knowledge of good and evil births judgment, which in turn demands justice. The curse is that in gaining that knowledge, man himself became guilty. They tried to cover the evidence by sewing aprons of fig leaves for themselves. It was the first of many things they would now struggle to provide for themselves through their own work.

Adam and his wife knew they were guilty. God had entrusted the garden to them, and they knew they had disobeyed. They knew God was coming, and they knew they deserved punishment. So they hid. But they misjudged God. God wasn't ignorant of what was going on, but despite that, He came into the garden looking for their regular time of fellowship. HaShem Elohim came to them as a parent, not as an offended king.

And they heard the sound of the LORD God walking in the garden in the cool of the day, and Adam and his wife hid themselves from the presence of the LORD God among the trees of the garden.

Then the LORD God called to Adam and said to him, "Where are you?"

So he said, "I heard Your voice in the garden, and I was afraid because I was naked; and I hid myself."

And He said, "Who told you that you were naked? Have you eaten from the tree of which I commanded you that you should not eat?"

Then the man said, "The woman whom You gave to be with me, she gave me of the tree, and I ate."

And the LORD God said to the woman, "What is this you have done?"

The woman said, "The serpent deceived me, and I ate." (Gen. 3:8–13)

Their awakened consciences condemned them. Who told them they were naked? They themselves did! *Naked* is a peculiar word that, especially with adults, carries a heavy dose of shame. If we only want to say someone is without clothes, we say *nude*. Shame conveys a sense of not meeting expectations, of being exposed as lacking, of being judged and found wanting. Here in the garden, even though God shows no displeasure or aggressiveness toward them, they hid. They were afraid, ashamed, and angry. Why do I say angry? Because they were embarrassed, acting out of self-preservation, justifying themselves, and shifting blame.

Adam blamed his wife; his wife blamed the serpent (Gen. 3:11–13).

Adam and Eve Are Self-Condemned

For most of us, this story of Adam and his wife, the garden, and the serpent's temptation is familiar. But let's look deeper into it. Where did all their embarrassment, guilt, self-justification, and blame-shifting suddenly come from?

We see that their consciences condemned them, but what in them, exactly, were their consciences condemning? It was themselves! This fact may appear obvious as we read, because this is the condition we were born into—but to Adam and his wife, this was new. Yes, their consciences were awakened, but this new activity in their consciences was a sign that something much more deadly had also awakened: a self-life, and all the entitlements it demanded.

When the serpent approached Eve, he tempted her with a choice. He did it subtly, by highlighting the one restriction put there by God, with no mention of the riches she already enjoyed in the garden. He tempted her to deny what she knew of the character of God and see Him as something else: a powerful, egocentric rule maker, not a father. The temptation was, *Make a choice for yourself.* The fruit was incidental. The serpent focused on the fruit because nothing else was forbidden in the garden. Other than for God's restriction, the fruit really was good for food (Gen. 2:16; 3:6). When Eve doubted God and paid attention to her physical senses, her physical and intellectual desires enticed her, and she ate. Then, meaning well, she shared this newly seen goodness with her husband, who knew better but didn't refuse.

So what immediately happened? They became not only self-conscious, but also ashamed. Those feelings hadn't been there before. They saw that they were naked. Their focus had suddenly turned inward. In a sense, they suddenly saw their own image and not God's. The serpent tempted them to become self-sufficient, and they couldn't do it. That's not how they were created or what they were created for. God had always provided, but now they saw their self-lack.

Their nakedness was shameful because the self hates being involuntarily exposed, especially by God. Nakedness was public, physical evidence of their failure. They shifted the blame because they'd lost their humility. Self is never wrong. They were ashamed, naked, angry, and afraid.

When the human's self was awakened, it was immediately at enmity with God. Self is the most powerful and stubborn anti-God force in the universe.

Adam and his wife could no longer think or see spiritual truths. They, like the serpent who had tempted them, became mastered by their physical desires. Their truth now came through their five senses and their emotions, and no longer from the words of God. As their self-life was born, their spirit-life, which had been in union with God, died. Because they had so radically changed, so did their world. Thus began the cursed inheritance that we, along with all mankind, received through Adam.

How was this new death to be conquered and real life restored?

CHAPTER 3

The Fruit of the Fruit of the Tree

He was in the world, and the world was made
through Him, and the world did not know
Him. He came to His own, and His own did not
receive Him.
John 1:10–11

**KEY: The knowledge of good and evil deceives a person
into believing he can see as the Creator sees.**

God's first question in Genesis 3 is: Where are you?
He came searching for Adam and his wife in the
garden. We should not read Genesis 3:9 as an accusation
or judgment, but as the first lament recorded in the Bible.
God's questions express the sorrow and disappointment of
a parent whose child has disobeyed: Where are you? What
have you done? Why have you left Me?

Adam had been placed in an idyllic existence in a garden created and planted just for him. God had provided
the perfect companion for him. He had everything he
needed, and he had dominion over it all (Gen. 1:26). His
only responsibility was to tend and keep the garden. Yet
when God, the owner of all and the one who had provided

everything for Adam appeared, Adam was afraid (Gen. 3:10).

We saw only half the picture when the woman ate from the tree, shared with her husband, and "the eyes of both of them were opened" (Gen. 3:6–7). Their eyes may have been newly opened, but their awareness was of their own nakedness. What we don't see immediately is that, although a new way of seeing had been opened, another part of them had died and become blind. They no longer recognized God's character and love for them. Instead, their new knowledge of good and evil convicted them; they knew they had disobeyed and fallen well short of God's requirements. Therefore, in their hearts, they knew punishment was both deserved and justified. The consequence of what they had done, just as God had warned them, was death. They could feel it, and for the first time in their lives, they were afraid. Adam and his wife hid while God searched for them. That same dysfunctional relationship persists in humankind to the present. Adam and his wife separated themselves from God. God did not separate Himself from them. God was not repelled by mankind's sin, nor did He reject mankind. To the contrary, He was grieved.

Even after God declared the consequences of their actions, He replaced their fig-leaf aprons and clothed them with coats (or tunics) of skin (Gen. 3:21). Although what God saw was still very good, because of their newborn sensitivities God accommodated Adam and Eve without blame and covered their shame.

Some people assume that since God made coverings of skin, an animal must have been killed and its blood shed; therefore, this must have been the first sacrifice for sin. That view is another not supported by the evidence here. First, neither animal nor blood nor sacrifice is mentioned in the passage. Second, that scenario would call for God to offer a sacrifice to . . . whom? Up to this point, everything had been brought into existence by a word of declaration from God or had been formed by God from the dust. Then natural reproduction took over. Would God have sacrificed something of His own creation to Himself? Genesis is unclear where the skin came from or even if a death was involved. The focus of the story is clearly not on the skin, but on God's compassion and love in covering their shame when their own poor efforts were embarrassingly inadequate.

Adam Names Eve

In the middle of this narrative between God making His pronouncement of consequences and God covering Adam and his wife with skins comes a verse that almost seems random: "And Adam called his wife's name Eve, because she was the mother of all living" (Gen. 3:20). Why did Adam choose this time to name his wife? Why didn't he name her, as he had all the animals, when he had first seen her? At that time all he said was, "She shall be called Woman, because she was taken out of Man" (Gen. 2:23). He classified her as to type, but not as to person. What was going on?

Adam had been given dominion over every living thing on the earth. When God brought all the animals to Adam to name (Gen. 2:19–20), Adam was not only looking for someone to complement him, but he was also taking the first steps of establishing his dominion. Ultimately that dominion would be established through his being fruitful, multiplying in numbers, subduing the earth, and managing it. But first, he was to manage—nurture, cultivate, and protect—the garden.

Interestingly, when the woman showed up, Adam did not name her. She is identified as his wife and "the woman" (because she came out of man). Remember, when Adam was created, God said, "Let Us make man in Our image, according to Our likeness; let them have dominion" (Gen. 1:26). After the woman came from man, the man continued to be called Adam, but the woman was nameless. I believe Adam didn't name her then because she had been in Adam when Adam was given dominion. When she was in Adam, the name of them both was Adam. Thus, they had been given dominion together.

The woman was created to be comparable to Adam, literally "a helper before him" (Gen. 2:18). She was not inferior to Adam in any way. In Hebrew, the word for *helper* used in Genesis 2:18 and 20 is *ezer* (pronounced ay-zer), and it is always and only used in the Old Testament in the context of vitally important and powerful acts of rescue and support. Adam's new wife was his equal but unique partner in his nurturing, cultivation, and dominion. She was strong and capable. Adam and his wife were to have been helpers together, cultivating and protecting each other, just as they were doing for the garden—increasing its life and beauty.

However, in tragic irony, the man and the woman who were meant to have dominion over all the creatures of the earth and all the trees of the garden were brought down by a sly serpent and a piece of fruit.

Adam's Sin

God addressed his "Where are you?" to Adam—the one who was tasked to care for and protect the garden (Gen. 2:15). Adam had been the first commissioned to rule and subdue (Gen. 1:28); he had been admonished to refrain from eating the fruit from a certain tree (Gen. 2:17). Adam was not vigilant in his stewardship, and he allowed the serpent's innuendos to prevail in Eve. Thus, the responsibility for the fall was Adam's. Adam was not deceived; the woman was (1 Tim. 2:14).

Adam was there at the scene of the crime, but he was passive. Genesis 3:6 shows Adam in proximity to his wife while she was conversing with the serpent. His presence was consistent with God's charge to him to tend and keep the garden. He was responsible for guarding the borders, but he failed to intervene when his wife was questioned. He failed in his responsibility to safeguard both the garden and his wife. Adam was responsible for this disaster because, through his passivity, he gave tacit approval to the serpent's insinuations. He was not deceived. The serpent, who had beguiled and deceived the woman, was absolutely guilty and deserved punishment, but the burden of responsibility for her deception was Adam's, for he had remained silent and had failed to exercise his authority and dominion.

But what was Adam's sin? We discussed how Eve had listened to the serpent and lost her trust in God as her loving father. Adam had heard the whole conversation. By dropping the name HaShem and leaving only Elohim when referring to God, the serpent was saying to them both, "God is not your parent; He is only your ruler and judge. Admit it. You're not obeying because you know He's a father who loves you; you're obeying because He commanded it. Admit it—you're obeying because He has power. Wouldn't you like some of that same power?"

Adam knowingly disobeyed. That's obvious. But why was the result of his disobedience so cataclysmic? I think we can see the answer in the life of the last Adam, Jesus, who came to redeem and restore what the first Adam had lost:

"For as the Father has life in Himself, so He has granted the Son to have life in Himself, and has given Him authority to execute judgment also, because He is the Son of Man" (John 5:26–27).

Human life emanates from the Father. When Adam disobeyed, he separated himself from his reliance on God the Father and relied on himself. He died since he had no life in himself.

Jesus, in contrast, lived His life dependent on Father God in a father-son relationship. He came that those who trust in Him could have life. His disciples are not just physically alive; they have the potential to live a superabundant life—a spilling-over life for the benefit of others also (John 10:10). This is one of those counterintuitive traps where we don't see clearly. We need to see that living our lives dependent on and in service to the Father, who is the very source of life and freedom, doesn't bring bondage—it brings life and freedom (Matt. 11:28–30).

Here's the dilemma: If you relate to God only because He's powerful, your thinking may go like this: *He's the pow-*

erful one, but I'm not convinced He loves me. From there, it's easy to become suspicious and think, *Maybe God is in this only for Himself.* The serpent fed that thought: God knows that if you eat, you'll be just like Him and won't have to worry about His motives. You can make your own decisions. You can't trust God.

You see, in a world where God is only Elohim, it is hard to serve God. Suspicions rise up and we think, *Who am I serving? He's powerful and He's in control, but does He truly have my interests at heart?*

The serpent's distortion of the truth was subtle. God did put a tree off-limits, but not to hoard His power. He did so out of love. He said, "Enjoy all the trees, while understanding that they're gifts. Know that you are beloved guests in My garden."

The two commandments go together to create the complete picture: eat from all the trees and avoid the other. When the commandments are separated, the serpent wins.

The Knowledge of Good and Evil

God had said that judging good and evil was His province alone. Although it's not a perfectly accurate perspective, it may help our understanding to think of God's creation as an elaborate role-playing game. Only the maker of the system, the creator, can be trusted to judge rightly. Why? The creator of the game is above the game. In this case, Adam and Eve are players in the game. God is not. He does not have a personal stake in the game like the players do. Only He can judge objectively because only He can see the whole scope of the game.

Adam, a player in the game, believing the lies of the

serpent about God's character, wanted the power of the Creator. In essence, he wanted the power of God to judge for himself whether God was good or evil. His great sin was not the disobedient act itself, but his rebellion behind the act—the thought that he could take the place of God— maybe not as the creator of the universe, but at least in running his own life.

The knowledge of good and evil gives you the feeling that you can see as the Creator does. But out of our own self-interest and bias, we confuse what we want to be for what should be in the world. We've all seen this. The most evil guy in the world doesn't see himself as evil. He thinks he's good, just misunderstood. In our post-Eden world, we can rationalize anything. That's why it's so hard to get out of an argument with someone. *How can I compromise if I believe my way is right? Why should I disrespect what I know to be truth just to get along with you?* We dress up our own opinions with truth, justice, and righteousness. However, as created beings we cannot be objective, and if our drive to make judgments isn't contained, it wrecks interpersonal relationships.

Once Adam and Eve bought into the serpent's lie that God is only Elohim and not HaShem Elohim, a terrible cascade of events unfolded. Deceived into believing that God was only powerful but not caring or compassionate to them as individuals, they turned their focus from a child-like innocence (Gen. 2:25) to a life of self-consciousness and self-preservation. When God confronted them with their sin, Adam blamed Eve and Eve blamed the serpent.

God's Curses Hold Hidden Blessings

What happened in this drama among the serpent, Adam, and his wife? The woman had been led by a creature, and the man had been led by his wife. As God declares the consequences of their actions here in Genesis chapter 3, I found that He removed the particular characteristic in each player that had been used for evil. The serpent became repulsive and lost its ability to openly approach people, especially women. The woman lost her self-sufficiency and became dependent, and Adam lost not only his provided-for position in the garden, but he also lost the special life God had breathed into him.

Those of us who have read the New Testament have a tremendous advantage when reading this passage because we have seen, and lived, its fulfillment. Therefore, the curses of God here are no longer puzzling. Rather, we can see they are the start of God's great plan of redemption for all people. Although there are immediate consequences for the serpent, Adam, and his wife, the pronouncements of God also foreshadow distant fulfillment when things shall be put right again.

> So the Lord God said to the serpent:
> "Because you have done this,
> You are cursed more than all cattle,
> And more than every beast of the field;
> On your belly you shall go,
> And you shall eat dust
> All the days of your life.
> And I will put enmity
> Between you and the woman,

> And between your seed and her Seed;
> He shall bruise your head,
> And you shall bruise His heel." (Gen. 3:14–15)

The Lord, the true judge, first pronounces sentence on the physical serpent. Note that the serpent is the only member of this trio that is specifically told it is being cursed. It is cursed more than every beast of the field. It becomes the type of all that is disgusting and low. The serpent, slithering in the dust and vulnerable to trampling, also becomes the symbol of Satan's humiliation and condemnation. In hindsight, we can see that God is not only speaking to the physical animal, but also to the spiritual serpent—the seducer.

"Between your seed and her Seed" (Gen. 3:15). The devil will have spiritual seed (John 8:44; Col. 3:6) and the woman—not Adam—will have one preeminent seed, thus foreshadowing the virgin birth of Christ. The serpent's poison is in its head, and that's where the Seed of the woman will strike the fatal blow—but it will be at the price of His pain and wounding by the devil's seed (Acts 2:23).

> To the woman He said:
>   "I will greatly multiply your sorrow and
> your conception;
>   In pain you shall bring forth children;
>   Your desire shall be for your husband,
>   And he shall rule over you." (Gen. 3:16)

The woman had taken the fruit and had given it to Adam. Adam had taken the fruit from his wife, knowing he was doing wrong. Why? We aren't told, but whatever the reason, in that moment Adam preferred his wife over God. He later blamed her—and God—for it (Gen. 3:12).

Now, standing before God, Eve can see what she started and the troubles she unleashed on herself and Adam. She will live in sorrow and regret ever after. Not only will she have physical pain in childbirth, but she will also have spiritual pain knowing the corrupted world she is bringing children into compared to the world that was. She is left in helpless torment as she's left with her regrets that she can now do nothing about.

She has lost the full trust of her husband, as Adam also now knows the enormity of his own disobedience aided by his wife. Although her desire for trusting intimacy still remains, the man will, in self-protection, rule over her. He will not heed the voice of his wife the same way again (Gen. 3:17).[5]

Finally, God comes to Adam:

> Then to Adam He said, "Because you have heeded the voice of your wife, and have eaten from the tree of which I commanded you, saying, 'You shall not eat of it':
> "Cursed is the ground for your sake;
> In toil you shall eat of it
> All the days of your life.
> Both thorns and thistles it shall bring forth for you,
> And you shall eat the herb of the field.
> In the sweat of your face you shall eat bread
> Till you return to the ground,
> For out of it you were taken;

> For dust you are,
> And to dust you shall return." (Gen. 3:17–19)

The cursing of the ground was not just that it started producing thorns and thistles, but also that it stopped being a struggle-free source of provision for Adam (Gen. 1:29), and instead changed into an ongoing judgment and curse against him (Gen. 8:21; Job 31:38–40; Rom. 8:20–22). Because the ground was part of the composition of man himself (Gen. 2:7), the curse of the ground became a power unto death working in Adam. Death was the wages of his sin (Rom. 6:23). Adam became mortal.

In human terms, God said to him, "Because you spurned My gifts and didn't follow the one rule of My garden, but instead wanted to be like Me, you can have what you wanted. Instead of having everything provided, you can take the raw materials I provide, you can grind your wheat, and you can produce something you can say you made—bread. You rejected My kind of life, so you can go back to where you came from—dust. You can have the consequences of what you've chosen."

The Way of Sin

In Eden, Adam and Eve had been living in a garden of God's grace. God had supplied all their needs, both directly and indirectly. The ground produced good food easily. They had satisfying responsibilities. There was open fellowship with God Himself without fear. But when Adam allowed himself to consider the serpent's poisonous insinuations about God and then acted based on those lies, he upended it all. "To him who knows to do good and does not do it, to him it is sin" (James 4:17). Adam was not deceived. He knew exactly what God wanted, but did the opposite.

The start of sin is subtle. The temptation always comes under the guise of personal autonomy. The serpent never said to Eve, "I want to be your master." The shift in allegiance is never from God to evil; it is always from God to self. Instead of His will, self-interest now rules, and what I want reigns. That is the essence of sin. The details of the story can distract us. In the end, it makes no difference who fed Adam or why he took the fruit. The command was, "Do not eat."

James 1:14–15 describes the downward spiral: "But each one is tempted when he is drawn away by his own desires and enticed. Then, when desire has conceived, it gives birth to sin; and sin, when it is full-grown, brings forth death." This is the path that Eve followed as she fell. Sin didn't come into the world through the serpent; it was conceived in the heart of man and matured into death.

Exile from the Garden

Sin is like a spiritual cancer. It may start as a minor blemish that's easily ignored or covered, but sin is corrosive. Eventually, like a cancer, it devours us by diverting needed energy and nutrients to feed itself instead of the body harboring it. We die of organ failure or starvation as we become less and less alive to the goodness of God.

God knew this. He had no concern of sin contaminating or hurting Himself, but He knew it would destroy human beings. So, in love, He removed them from the situation where their condition would become irreversible. God had to separate Adam and Eve from the Tree of Life and remove them from Eden.

> "Behold, the man has become like one of Us, to know good and evil. And now, lest he put out his hand and take also of the tree of life, and eat, and live forever"—therefore the LORD God sent him out of the garden of Eden to till the ground from which he was taken. (Gen. 3:22–23)

These words were not spoken in anger or irony as is generally supposed, but in deep compassion. "The words should be rendered, 'Behold, what has become [by sin] of the man who was as one of us!' Formed, at first, in our image to know good and evil—how sad his condition now."[6]

Adam and Eve, by losing their understanding of God as their loving parent and seeing Him only as a powerful ruler, had already in their hearts and emotions left the garden. They no longer wanted to walk with God. Their job of dressing and keeping the garden would have become a burden as their efforts would no longer come out of love and delight, but out of duty and fear of God's power.

Some wonder why Adam and Eve hadn't already eaten from the Tree of Life since they had been in the garden so long with free access to that tree. I believe there had been no temptation to do so. For the first temptation, the serpent had to present the temptation to Eve. She had no innate desire to eat from the forbidden tree. The idea came from outside her. Only after the fall did other temptations arise from mankind's own internal desires (James 1:14), and an external tempter was no longer necessary. Additionally, since they were already filled with God's breath of life (Gen. 2:7), eating from the Tree of Life would have added no benefit to them. But now, having fallen and no longer drawing their life from God, the temptation of the tree would be overwhelming. They wanted independence, self-sufficiency, and power. Having control over life itself, in their twisted thinking, would make them like gods.

"So He drove out the man; and He placed cherubim at the east of the garden of Eden, and a flaming sword which turned every way, to guard the way to the tree of life" (Gen. 3:24). Note that the Tree of Life still exists and there is still a way, but now it's guarded by cherubim. The way back is not blocked, but it's guarded. The Tree of Life is preserved, and we will see the figures of these cherubim again in our story.

I particularly like how one commentary explains that although the garden-life was closed to Adam and Eve, God provided a new path to life for all humankind:

> [Genesis 3:24] should be rendered thus: "And he dwelt between the cherubim at the East of the Garden of Eden and a fierce fire, or Shekinah, unfolding itself to preserve the way of the tree of life." This was the mode of worship now established to show God's anger at sin and teach the mediation of a promised Saviour as the way of life, as well as of access to God. They were the same figures as were afterwards in the tabernacle and temple; and now, as then, God

said, "I will commune with thee from above
the mercy seat, from between the two cheru-
bims" (Exodus 25:22).[7]

The wonderful paradox here is in the way God provided escape. In removing Adam and Eve from the Tree of
Life, God made it possible that, in the fullness of time, we
could have real life again. It will be new life from a different
tree, featuring a different Adam (1 Cor. 15:45–49; 1 Peter
2:24; Rom. 6:4), and death itself will be swallowed up in
victory (1 Cor. 15:54).

Adam and Eve were evicted by God from the garden
with no way to go back, but God won't keep them separated from Him.

CHAPTER 4

Adam's Legacy through His Children

*Each one is tempted when he is drawn away by
his own desires and enticed. Then, when desire
has conceived, it gives birth to sin; and sin, when
it is full-grown, brings forth death.*
James 1:14–15

KEY: The first Adam's lineage forfeits the likeness of God.

God drove Adam and Eve from the garden. Although their relationship had changed, there's no hint that God was angry. Adam had been brought to the garden by HaShem Elohim. The garden was a place for His children to delight in and where God could spend time with them, each learning to know the other. It was God's garden, created as a beautiful and fruitful place for His children. A father lives in the house with his children, while a king lives in a palace with his subjects outside. Once Adam and Eve made the decision to see God as only Elohim, only as the almighty king, they had to live outside.

Although they had disobeyed God and had chosen death instead of life, God was not leaving them. However, their interrelationship had been badly damaged. Meetings with God now held an element of fear. Because of their experience with the tree, they now judged for themselves what God told them to see whether it seemed good to them. They and their offspring became more easily offended at being told what to do.

The same new attitude of judging applied to the relationship between Adam and Eve. They were no longer equals now that Adam, rather than God, ruled over Eve. Compounding the problem, her desire was for her husband, who couldn't perfectly meet all her needs. Because of her experience with the tree, she couldn't help but judge her husband's actions and decisions. And overarching it all, everything they accomplished required pain, sorrow, and the sweat of their brows. What a mix for ongoing stress, resentment, and blaming!

Adam and Eve were not under a curse from God; they were cursed by the consequences of their own choice. God was still involved in their lives and still loved them.

Time passed and Adam and Eve had children: two boys. First Cain, then Abel. As they grew, Cain became a dirt farmer growing food, while Abel became a shepherd keeping the animals. At a certain time, they both decided to bring an offering to the Lord. The passage in Genesis 4 doesn't say if this was a requirement from God or not, but apparently there were criteria for what was acceptable and what was not. Cain offered "the fruit of the ground." Abel brought "of the first lambs of the year and of their fat." They presented their offerings. The Hebrew word used here for *offering* refers to a presentation that is usually both bloodless and voluntary, in contrast to the word used for *sacrifice*. The Lord respected Abel and his offering, but He did not respect Cain and his offering (Gen. 4:4–5).

Cain Is Offended

We're not told why Cain's offering was not respected, and that question is outside the focus of this book. It is clear that when Cain brought his offering, Cain himself judged it acceptable. However, God did not respect Cain's assessment of his gift, so Cain got angry because his judgment was found deficient. We need to look at Cain's reaction:

> Cain was very angry, and his countenance fell. So the LORD said to Cain, "Why are you angry? And why has your countenance fallen? If you do well, will you not be accepted? And if you do not do well, sin lies at the door. And its desire is for you, but you should rule over it." (Gen. 4:5–7)

Cain felt angry and rejected—the perfect time for sin to attack. Instead of getting angry in return, God counseled Cain: "Just do well and you will be accepted. Follow My directions, and things will go well for you" (Gen. 4:7). God warned Cain that he was standing at a decision point. If he chose not to do well and not to follow God's instructions, sin, like an animal, was at his heart's door and wanted to consume him. God also identified the way out: "You must rule over it." Cain did not rule over his anger, nor did he want to. He judged that he had been treated unfairly and had been "shown up" before God by his brother Abel.

> Now Cain talked with Abel his brother; and it came to pass, when they were in the field, that Cain rose up against Abel his brother and killed him.
>
> Then the LORD said to Cain, "Where is Abel your brother?"
>
> He said, "I do not know. Am I my brother's keeper?"
>
> And He said, "What have you done? The voice of your brother's blood cries out to Me from the ground. So now you are cursed from the earth, which has opened its mouth to receive your brother's blood from your hand. When you till the ground, it shall no longer yield its strength to you. A fugitive and a vagabond you shall be on the earth."
>
> And Cain said to the LORD, "My punishment is greater than I can bear! Surely You have driven me out this day from the face of the ground; I shall be hidden from Your face; I shall be a fugitive and a vagabond on the earth, and it will happen that anyone who finds me will kill me."
>
> And the LORD said to him, "Therefore, whoever kills Cain, vengeance shall be taken on him sevenfold." And the LORD set a mark on Cain, lest anyone finding him should kill him. (Gen. 4:8–15)

Let's look closer at several things here. Cain killed his brother in an act of premeditated murder. He did not act out of passion. Even after God warned him to control his emotions, he talked with his brother, and then later, when they were alone, Cain "rose up against Abel" and killed him. The Lord talked to Cain again, asking him where his brother was. Notice that Cain was neither surprised nor intimidated by the presence of God. Talking with God was both an expected and usual occurrence for him. In fact, Cain was so comfortable with God (and still angry) that he first lied to God: "I don't know where he is." Then he responded with sarcasm: "Am I my brother's keeper?"

Cain felt no shame or guilt. He felt that what he had done was just. As we've noted previously, having the knowledge of good and evil gives the illusion that you see as the Creator sees. Therefore, we confuse what we want in our world for what should be in our world. Acting on your desire always seems in the moment like the right thing to do. After all, you have the knowledge (but not the objectivity or wisdom) of God.

Thus, in Cain's heart, Cain *knew* his offering was acceptable. *It was wrong of God not to accept it.* Cain also knew Abel's offering was not as good as his. *It certainly hadn't taken as much work. But God accepted Abel's offering and Abel was favored. Totally unjust!*

Remember that God used the knowledge of good and evil to judge whether something should remain in His creation or not. In the same way, Cain judged Abel and his actions as evil. They were a constant reminder of Cain's own falling short of God's standard. He was labeled inadequate when he *knew* he was more. Therefore, Abel had to be removed from Cain's world. Murder, in Cain's heart, was justified.

Cain had been a farmer, but God tells him he will be cursed from the earth, which had received Abel's blood. The ground was cursed already because of Adam, and now the ground itself cursed Cain. He would find it even more difficult, if not impossible, to coax any yield from the soil. Because he will have no workable land, he is forced to be a vagabond and wanderer. He has suddenly lost his identity. The one thing he had done well was now shut off from him. He laments to God that because he has been driven from the face of the earth, he will also be hidden from God's face. God has said nothing about hiding His face from Cain, but Cain's world was getting darker as he made choices that took him away from God's presence. The change was happening in Cain, not God.

Cain was sent away from the land and from the work he knew well. He had lost God's favor by rejecting God's ways. He had had choices, but his desires and sin condemned him. Sin had conquered him, blinded him, and deadened him to God (1 John 2:9–11). Cain's descendants continued to avoid agriculture and instead built cities, engaged in manufacturing, and pursued music.

Two Bloodlines

Adam and Eve had another son and named him Seth, which means *appointed* or *put*, and they looked on him as "another seed . . . instead of Abel" (Gen. 4:25). Unlike Adam, who had been created in God's image and after His likeness (Gen. 1:26), Seth was identified as a son in Adam's own likeness and after his image (Gen. 5:3). He was physically like Adam, and his character was like Adam's. In Adam, all die. It will be in Christ, who in His humanity was in the lineage of Seth, that humankind will be reborn into a new lineage, free from bondage to sin (1 Cor. 15:21–22).

This was the great divergence in the offspring of Adam and Eve, and therefore of all humanity. Cain left his homeland and followed his own wisdom, wandering, spiritually blind, wherever he thought best. The line of Cain was effectively lost to history after the seventh generation.

The line of Adam through Seth continued for nine generations until Noah. Seth's lineage was characterized by producing families, as opposed to Cain's line who produced *things*. After Seth's son Enos was born, the Bible notes, "Then men began to call on the name of the LORD" (Gen. 4:26). They were calling on the name of HaShem (Yahweh) and not Elohim alone.

Calling on the name of the Lord is not just voicing the word, but is primarily an act of submission and humility. To call on someone else acknowledges one's need and asks for someone greater to help. This entreaty for another's care is not only a time of petition, but is also an act of worship and an acknowledgment of lordship. God honors and respects that kind of offering.

What a difference in the trajectories of these two bloodlines! Cain's illustrated the truth of Proverbs 14:12: "There is a way that seems right to a man, but its end is the way of death."

In contrast, God continued to favor Seth's line because

his heirs continued to position themselves to be favored. They chose to "do well," as God had counseled Cain to do. They called on the name of the Lord, and they built families, in contrast to Cain's retort, "Am I my brother's keeper?" Many years later, the prophet Joel prophesied of Seth's descendants, "And it shall come to pass that whoever calls on the name of the LORD shall be saved" (Joel 2:32).

It's a caution to all of us that it was these apparently small, spontaneous choices that determined family destinies for centuries. To Adam, the question was, "Where are you?" and to Cain, "Where is Abel, your brother?" Adam faced the question directly and said, "I was afraid because I was naked and I hid." But then he went to God, who covered him.

Cain, however, was annoyed at being questioned. God had no respect for his offering, and Cain showed no respect for God. "Why are You asking me? I don't know where my brother is, and why am I supposed to, anyway?" Even after God told him his fate, Cain didn't repent. He feared only for his self-preservation. Yet God provided for him, even in his rebellion.

CHAPTER 5

The Problem with Sin

*Whoever loves instruction and correction
loves knowledge, but he who hates reproof is
like a brute beast, stupid and
indiscriminating.*
Proverbs 12:1 AMPCE

KEY: The life of God is incompatible with sin.

The serpent convinced Adam and Eve they would gain something valuable when they ate the forbidden fruit. The fruit held the promise of godlike wisdom. While God named it the Tree of the Knowledge of Good and Evil, when Eve looked on it, she saw that the tree was "desirable to make one wise" (Gen. 3:6). However, it was the Tree of the *Knowledge* of Good and Evil. She was deceived, and her interpretation of what she was seeing was wrong. A truly wise person will tell you that increasing your knowledge does not increase your wisdom. True wisdom in this case would have been to obey God and not eat the fruit. True wisdom in *any* case is to obey God (Prov. 9:10).

What's the difference between humans and animals? More specifically, what was the difference between the serpent and Eve? The serpent walked, talked, apparently liked good food, and was extremely intelligent. Adam and Eve also walked, talked, admired and appreciated good food, and were extremely intelligent.

The obvious answer is in Genesis 2:7: "The LORD God formed man of the dust of the ground, and breathed into his nostrils the breath of life; and man became a living being." Humans had God's breath of life, while the animals did not. But is there anything else making a difference?

Traditional Jewish interpretation of the serpent's question provides an intriguing perspective. The question, read literally in Hebrew, says, "Even if God [*Elohim*] told you not to eat from any of the trees in the garden . . ." (Gen. 3:1), and the sentence dies away. The key to understanding this is seeing the emphasis on the word *told*.

The serpent was a beast of the field, and therefore had a beast's perspective. Assuming the serpent was speaking the truth from its perspective, we now see the temptation as, "Even if God *told* you not to eat of every tree of the garden . . . [do it anyway!]."

How does this work? Animals were created with internal instructions. Absent outside influence—such as training or domestication—they survive by following their instincts. Good or evil does not exist within them; theirs is a life of desire versus lack of desire.

Humans were different from the beginning. God gave Adam external instructions through His words; he was to be guided by the commands of God (Gen. 2:16–17), not by his internal appetites.

So what was the serpent saying? According to this traditional view, which may sound strange to modern Christians, but offers fascinating insight, the serpent is saying, "It doesn't matter what God *told* you to do. What matters is what you *want* to do. That's how it works for me. What are your gut instincts telling you?"[8]

Both Adam and Eve heard this talk. Eve reached out, took the fruit, and shared with Adam. She did what she judged was good for her. They gave in to their own newly awakened desires and threw aside the command of God.

This same animal-like desire was alive within Cain and may well have been the sin crouching at the door for him and calling to him. Unfortunately, his passion and anger drove him through the door to sin, and it controlled him. If instead he had controlled his desires and had done as God told him, he would have been saved from his fate (Gen. 4:7). The escape was in his "doing well."

The woman ate the fruit only after she looked at it and gave in to her desires. She did what she judged was good for her. Adam named her Eve after their fall. She was "the mother of all living," and all future humanity would come through her. However, their children would no longer bear the image of God, but rather the image of Adam (Gen 5:3).

In contrast, Mary, the mother of Jesus, the "last Adam" (1 Cor. 15:45), surrendered her desires and preferences to God, saying, "Behold the maidservant of the Lord! Let it be to me according to your word" (Luke 1:38). Because of her yielding to God's plan instead of her own, not only was she blessed, but all the nations of the earth were blessed through her. Eve chose the way of death; Mary chose the way of life. Both received the consequences of their choice.

Adam and Eve made an independent, moral choice against God's directive. They chose to follow their own desires instead of God's instructions. This thinking is so common today that we easily miss its destructive significance. Adam and Eve made a conscious, deliberate choice to serve their own desire and, thereby, not serve God. The apostle Paul explains it succinctly in his letter to the Romans: "Do you not know that to whom you present yourselves slaves to obey, you are that one's slaves whom you obey, whether of sin leading to death, or of obedience leading to righteousness?" (Rom. 6:16). We, through Adam, became slaves to sin. As his heirs, our instinct is to rule ourselves, and our original spirit connection with God is dead. Adam had no life, other than his own, to pass to his children. Human wills became skewed and corrupted as our divine orientation was lost. We became self-centered instead of God-focused. Instead of living the abundant, joy-filled, purposeful life we were made for, our destiny became death.

Although sin is insidious and deadly, it is almost universally underestimated. We have been trained to look at sin primarily in legal terms, such as breaking one of the Ten Commandments. *Sins* (plural) are seen as wrong acts that we do, while the more important root, *sin* (singular), tends to be ignored since it's not visible. However, God sees it differently. James says "When desire has conceived, it gives birth to sin; and sin, when it is full-grown, brings forth death" (James 1:15). This description doesn't distinguish between big sins and little sins. That's not the issue. The Bible identifies the problem as *sin*, singular.

Jesus came into the world preannounced as the Savior.

Savior from what? When His birth was first announced to Joseph, the angel said, "You shall call His name Jesus, for He will save His people from their sins" (Matt. 1:21). He will save them *from* their sins. That is much more significant and thorough than forgiving people *for* their sins, although Jesus also accomplished that. John 3:16 says that He saves us from the path of perishing that we're on and gives everlasting life.

Jesus came into this world free from sin (2 Cor. 5:21). His light revealed the extent of the ravages of sin in our lives. Mankind was blind and on the wrong path to God. When Jesus said that no one knows the Father except the Son (Matt. 11:27; Luke 10:22), His words exposed our delusion that all was well with our relationship with God if we just kept the commandments—followed the rules. But sin is a much larger problem than breaking a few rules. In other words, if eternal life is knowing the Father, as Jesus said in John 17:3, then eternal death is not knowing the Father, and sin is the cause of our not knowing.

Sin Closes the Eyes of Our Understanding

When Adam and Eve sinned, the great disaster wasn't that they broke a divine rule, and therefore they were going to be rejected. When they listened to the serpent and believed his lie, they became blind. Obviously, they weren't physically blind, but their perception of spiritual reality became dark. They could no longer perceive the truth about God or themselves. That's why they hid from God when He came looking for them. Nothing had changed about God, but they had changed. God still saw them without shame and still desired fellowship with them, but they saw themselves much differently. They saw themselves as naked and deserving of punishment.

If we were created to find our life, purpose, and delight in the Father, then becoming blind to Him is our greatest disaster.

If God is not known as loving, trustworthy, and faithful, then individuals are driven to become sufficient in themselves. Pride soon follows.

Everyone since the garden has been affected. Look at God's description of the people in one of the churches in the book of Revelation: "I know your works. . . . You say, 'I am rich, have become wealthy, and have need of nothing'—and do not know that you are wretched, miserable, poor, blind, and naked" (Rev. 3:15, 17). What irony that this is the same pattern we saw in Genesis! Adam and Eve thought they were gaining the last piece they needed to be happy, healthy, and wise; instead, they woke up to their newfound blindness, nakedness, and lack. Their desire to be like God became their misery.

God stands with humankind, yet remains above humanity. He never left or abandoned humans. He gives each person a choice to follow Him or to do what is right in their own eyes. As we saw with Cain, one choice leads to life, while the other leads to death and destruction. Sin has always been about making choices against not only the will of God, but also against God Himself. Sin darkens understanding and leads away from wisdom. However wise one may seem in his own eyes, such wisdom is foolishness in God's perspective. It is foolish because it leads to destruction. The door to life is open, and choosing another way is suicidal. As God said to Cain, "If you do well, will you not be accepted?"

In Revelation, God said, "I know your works." Actions reveal what's in the heart. At first glance, it may seem that all we need is a good behavior modification program to teach us how we can consistently "do well," but that would only deal with symptoms. Sin is much deeper than that and has already twisted our hearts. Jeremiah 17:9 says, "The heart is deceitful above all things, and desperately wicked; who can know it?" *Desperately wicked* in this passage can also be translated "incurably sick"—a strange delusional sickness that makes you feel strong, independent, and self-sufficient, even while you're dying cold, alone, and in rags. Only God can cure this sickness, but only through death.

CHAPTER 6

The Grace of Obedience

Do not be wise in your own eyes;
Fear the LORD and depart from evil.
It will be health to your flesh,
And strength to your bones.
Proverbs 3:7–8

KEY: Obedience is evidence of being on the road to restoration.

The healing path for humankind is paved with faith and obedience. Hebrews 11:6 tells us that without faith, it is impossible to please God. However, throughout history, from creation through God's dealings with His people, Israel, and even in the teachings of Jesus, there's an emphasis on obedience. Why? So how does keeping the law please God if God is only pleased by faith? Where is the faith if people are just blindly following a list of instructions?

Hebrews 11:6 goes on to answer that question: "He who comes to God must believe that He is, and that He is a rewarder of those who diligently seek Him." First, the people must recognize who is behind the laws and must realize they are there for their freedom and not their bondage. Second, the people must recognize that there is reward in doing well. Seeing God behind the laws and obeying them out of reverence and confident trust in His goodness was the evidence of their faith.

Hebrews chapter 11 goes on to list the heroes of the faith from Abel through the prophets and beyond. One thing distinguished them all. They acted contrary to their natural instincts and instead acted as God directed them. In other words, they did what the Person they said they had faith in told them to do. That's what faith is. They acted on His words; they didn't act like beasts.

This is also how Jesus walked. He was guided from the outside in, from His Father, and not from His own desires. He lived a life of obedience. "Most assuredly, I say to you, the Son can do nothing of Himself, but what He sees the Father do; for whatever He does, the Son also does in like manner" (John 5:19).

We must live the same way as Jesus lived if we are to share in God's life. Humankind is handicapped by its broken concepts of God and its natural self-centered desires. Thus the working out of our salvation—the practical living of it—is centered on obedience and discipline. Concerning sin, the principle is the same as it was with Cain: it's control yourself or be controlled.

> Therefore, my beloved, as you have always obeyed, not as in my presence only, but now much more in my absence, work out your own salvation with fear and trembling; for it is God who works in you both to will and to do for His good pleasure.

> Do all things without complaining and
> disputing, that you may become blameless and
> harmless, children of God without fault in the
> midst of a crooked and perverse generation,
> among whom you shine as lights in the world,
> holding fast the word of life. (Phil. 2:12–16)

Am I describing a salvation by works? No! It's all by faith. Works by themselves mean little. The motivation for the works must be an outflow of faith. Faith is choosing to follow God's ways instead of our desires. Living by faith requires dying to the self's desires and deferring to God. We cede the right to judge good and evil back where it belongs—to God alone. We connect to the grace and mercy of God through our faith in Christ. A living faith in Jesus always changes how we live.

We must believe in Jesus practically, in the same way as He believed in His Father. We cannot follow Him only theoretically, by holding "this or that theory about why He died or wherein lay His atonement: such things can be revealed only to those who follow Him in His active being and the principle of His life—who do as He did, live as He lived. There is no other [kind of] following."[9]

But obedience is a sensitive subject, so before we go further, I need to talk about what the Bible means by obedience. My natural reaction to being told I must obey is offended pride. Alarms go off, and I feel that my freedom is being taken away. I am being bent to someone else's will. The very idea feels stifling and limiting. Obedience feels as if a set of external requirements is being imposed upon me, along with penalties for not obeying. And ironically, even if I willingly obey, I still have a sense of restriction and a contrary desire to quickly get back to the point where I can be left alone so I can do things myself again without supervision.

But since I want to be a good Christian, my tendency is to sigh and say, "OK, give me the list of rules and I'll do my best." Adam and Eve had one commandment. Noah introduced seven, and through Moses the number went up to 613! We always want the list so we can judge how we're doing—or so we say. More often we use the list to check how we're doing compared to others. But God says obedience is not about doing the list. It's about relationship (Matt. 7:21–23).

Adam was created after the likeness of God; our whole being was originally tuned to live in fellowship and harmony with Him (John 5:19). Therefore, when we think about obedience, God's commandments should not be viewed as impositions into our freedom from an outside will, but as revelation of how to best live the unimpeded life and freedom we were made for—they keep us in tune with God. Why do I say revelation? Because our view of both God's character and our needs were distorted by sin; we couldn't see clearly. For example, telling the owner of a high-performance automobile that he shouldn't use regular grade gasoline, but only a higher-grade premium, will ultimately lead to his freedom and not be his limitation. Only an ignorant driver would grumble at that apparent restriction. But that's exactly what we used to be: ignorant.

True Humility

The obedience that God rewards is rooted in humility. God not only observes our behavior, but He also knows the motivation of our heart. Humble obedience is a deliberate deference on our part, acknowledging a higher wisdom, plan, and purpose than ours. This obedience is not forced on us from outside, but is an outworking of our own contented decision to abdicate our self-rule, renounce our throne, and submit to a new Lord and culture. The obedience we now exhibit doesn't come from external threats, but out of a deep understanding that we serve a Lord greater than ourselves who loves us and is a rewarder of those who perseveringly follow Him (Heb. 11:6). God doesn't force our obedience; we give it willingly. To do otherwise is ignorant and foolish because "by humility and the fear of the LORD are riches and honor and life" (Prov. 22:4).

Humility, at its most basic, is having a sober view of our position and not thinking more highly of ourselves and our opinions than we ought to think (Rom. 12:3). It is deferring to God in matters of what is and what is not truth. It is found in the wisdom of following His direction over our own desires, without offense or resentment. Jesus said, "If anyone loves Me, he will keep My word; and My Father will love him, and We will come to him and make Our home with him. He who does not love Me does not keep My words" (John 14:23–24). He described the situation in a parable contrasting the results from wise and foolish builders—the humble contrasted with the proud:

> But why do you call Me "Lord, Lord," and not do the things which I say? Whoever comes to Me, and hears My sayings and does them, I will show you whom he is like: He is like a man building a house, who dug deep and laid the foundation on the rock. And when the flood

arose, the stream beat vehemently against
that house, and could not shake it, for it was
founded on the rock. But he who heard and
did nothing is like a man who built a house on
the earth without a foundation, against which
the stream beat vehemently; and immediately
it fell. And the ruin of that house was great.
(Luke 6:46–49)

Faith is necessary to please God, and righteous works
are the outflow of a living faith. Works not done from faith,
no matter how righteous they appear, are dead. Those kinds
of works are all too familiar to us; they are the works that
have become a burden or merely an obligation. They don't
flow out of faith, but are done out of fear, duty, or for the
sake of appearance. They are not from faith, and "whatever
is not from faith is sin" (Romans 14:23). Why are they sin?
Because the motivation for our works shifts from God to
ourselves. It is the pattern of Cain and his offering. When
works are not vitalized by faith, they are cut off from God,
who is life. Anything not coming from life is death.

Still, my natural inclination was not to consider the
law either something to be delighted in or a source of joy.
But King David, in the first Psalm, said that anyone who
delights in God's law is blessed. David saw the law as God
saw it: as the path to life and prosperity. It was his source of
wisdom and comfort and his guard against deception (Ps.
119:97–105).

God's ways, God's laws, are His blessing. The choice is
put before us. We are the ones who make our way prosper-
ous (Josh. 1:8). The fear of the Lord may be the beginning

of wisdom (Prov. 9:10), but humility and obedience are wisdom in action. God's ways produce peace, long life, favor, honor, purpose, health, and understanding! Our own ways may seem right, but they are the ways of death (Prov. 14:12).

Obedience to God is not volunteering for a new prison of bondage with a different warden. It is the journey of life through the renewing of our minds unto the salvation of our souls through faith (Rom. 12:2; Heb. 10:37–11:1).

CHAPTER 7

Israel, Our Example

For it is not merely hearing the Law [read] that
makes one righteous before God, but it is the
doers of the Law who will be held guiltless and
acquitted and justified.
Romans 2:13 AMPCE

KEY: The virulence of sin is restrained by the law.

From the time of Eden, God continued to woo humanity back into a harmonious relationship with Himself. But man, with his warped human will, resisted. A few followed God, but the majority chose to trust in themselves. By the time of Noah, all the people on earth had been free for centuries to make their own choices, and they were doing whatever was right in their own eyes. God's assessment was "that the wickedness of man was great in the earth, and that every intent of the thoughts of his heart was only evil continually" (Gen. 6:5).

"But Noah found grace in the eyes of the LORD" (Gen. 6:8). God instructed him to build an ark that saved him and his family from the great flood that killed all life on land (Gen. 7:21–23). According to Hebrews 11:7, it was through this obedience that Noah "became heir of the righteousness which is according to faith."

God Reestablishes Relationship through Covenant

Beginning with Noah, through his son Shem, God laid the foundation for a great nation, one that was to live in covenant relationship with Him. God had initiated a covenant with Noah after the flood and renewed it with his descendant Abram (Gen. 17:7). This covenant incorporated the sign of circumcision, a cutting away of flesh—significantly, from the only part of the body that has anything to do with being fruitful and multiplying. As part of the covenant, Abram's name was changed to Abraham, and his wife's name was changed from Sarai to Sarah. The new names meant, respectively, "Father of Many Nations" and "Princess" (to many).

A name exchange is always part of entering into covenant. Each person takes on the name of the other family or tribe as a part of the process. Echoes of the practice come down to us today in marriage as, traditionally, the bride takes the groom's name. Notice that Abram took on a sound, *ha*, from God's name, while God started calling Himself "the God of Abraham," and later, as the covenant was extended, the "God of Abraham, Isaac, and Jacob." Thus, each time the new name was voiced, Abram was saying, "I am Abraham, in covenant with God," and God was saying, "I am God, in covenant with Abraham." The naming process, as we saw in Eden, was a sign of dominion. Here Abram submits to God, but God also pledges loyalty back to Abram.

After this covenant was established and after Abraham had been circumcised in obedience:

- He and Sarah had their first and only son together—Isaac;
- Isaac had a son named Jacob;
- The covenant of Abraham was renewed with Abraham's son, Isaac, and later, with Isaac's son, Jacob (Gen. 26, 28);
- Jacob wrestled with God one night and prevailed. He was given the name Israel, meaning "a Prince of God" or "God [El] Fights" (Gen. 32:28, 30);
- Jacob (Israel) had twelve sons, "the children of Israel"; and
- from them came the physical nation of Israel.

The Covenant Continues in Israel through Moses

Famine came to the land during Jacob's time, and through a series of events, his whole family moved to Egypt, where there was food and favor for them—until there was a change of pharaohs. Then the whole nation became enslaved.

God raised up Moses, miraculously saving him from the king's decree to kill all male babies at birth. Instead, Moses was adopted by the king's daughter and was raised in the palace and trained as an Egyptian, both culturally and militarily.

As an adult, Moses identified with the Hebrews. One day he saw an Egyptian beating an Israelite. Moses killed the Egyptian, thereby incurring the anger of Pharaoh. Because of that failed rescue attempt, Moses had to flee for his life to the land of Midian, where he stayed forty years and created a new life for himself.

Eventually that pharaoh died, and a new pharaoh succeeded him. After almost forty years—after Moses felt that he was safe and would never have to worry about Egypt again, God found Moses. As he was tending sheep, Moses saw a bush burning, but it was not being consumed by the flames. After Moses's curiosity was piqued, and God saw that he had turned his attention from the flock to the bush, God spoke to Moses out of the bush, introducing Himself as the God of his father—of Abraham, of Isaac, and of Jacob. He said:

> I have surely seen the oppression of my people who are in Egypt, and have heard their cry because of their taskmasters, for I know their sorrows. . . . Come now, therefore, and I will send you to Pharaoh that you may bring my people, the children of Israel, out of Egypt. (Ex. 3:7, 10)

We know the ensuing story—of the exodus, of the ten plagues, of crossing the Red Sea on dry ground, and the destruction of the Egyptian army. Moses, this time acting in obedience to God, successfully led the Israelites out of Egyptian bondage and toward hope and promise in a new land (Ex. 5–15).

God's Great Offer to Israel

A little more than two months after they left Egypt, the Israelites came to Mount Sinai, where God made them a magnificent proposal:

> And Moses went up to God, and the LORD called to him from the mountain, saying, "Thus you shall say to the house of Jacob, and tell the children of Israel: 'You have seen what I did to the Egyptians, and how I bore you on eagles' wings and brought you to Myself. Now therefore, if you will indeed obey My voice and keep My covenant, then you shall be a special treasure to Me above all people; for all the earth is Mine. And you shall be to Me a kingdom of priests and a holy nation.'" (Ex. 19:3–6)

If the people would obey God's voice and keep covenant with Him, Israel would be a kingdom of priests. In other words, God was offering each person a personal relationship with Him.

Moses came down from the mountain and told the people the proposal. They agreed to those requirements and said, "All that the LORD has spoken we will do." Moses told God what the people had said, and God told Moses to have the people consecrate themselves for three days.

> Then it came to pass on the third day, in the morning, that there were thunderings and lightnings, and a thick cloud on the mountain; and the sound of the trumpet was very loud, so

> that all the people who were in the camp trembled. And Moses brought the people out of the camp to meet with God, and they stood at the foot of the mountain. (Ex. 19:16–17)

Moses brought the people out of the camp to meet with God, but this time they were so terrified at what they were seeing and hearing that they backed away from the mountain and told Moses that he could do all the speaking to God and then relay the information to them. Their hearts again deceived them, as they were terrified that if God spoke directly to them, they would die. God had offered them unique and personal status with Himself, but they rejected it, even while they watched Moses interact with God and live. While they stood away in fear, they heard God verbally give the Ten Commandments.

> Now all the people witnessed the thunderings, the lightning flashes, the sound of the trumpet, and the mountain smoking; and when the people saw it, they trembled and stood afar off. Then they said to Moses, "You speak with us, and we will hear; but let not God speak with us, lest we die."
>
> And Moses said to the people, "Do not fear; for God has come to test you, and that His fear may be before you, so that you may not sin." So the people stood afar off, but Moses drew near the thick darkness where God was. (Ex. 20:18–21)

The people were struck with terror at the presence of God. Moses said, "God is providing deliverance for you that you may not sin. He wants you to remember this experience so you will have motivation not to sin. Don't be afraid; this is good, not bad. You'll see that this is the Lord who loves you, who delivered you out of Egypt and out of bondage [Ex. 20:2]. Have faith and obey."

Unfortunately, the God Moses knew and was urging them toward was not the God they saw in front of them. Their sin distorted their perception, and they were terrified.

So Moses, at the people's demand, became a mediator between God and the people of Israel. God will come as close to us as we will let Him.

The Israelites Commit Themselves to God

Moses knew God and talked regularly with Him while the Israelites watched, stayed dependent on Moses, and didn't understand. As Psalm 103:7 puts it, "He made known His ways to Moses, His acts to the children of Israel." All the Israelites had vowed, "All that the LORD has spoken we will do" (Ex. 19:8). Receiving the law was a significant step in God's bringing His people's hearts back to Himself.

The children of Israel knew the acts of God, such as their miraculous deliverance from Egypt and provision of food and water in the desert, but they didn't know God Himself. Living under the law, with all its required observances, and having the tabernacle in the middle of their camp, moved their focus to God and began to teach them His ways, even if it was only in shadow. Still, it was enough for them to be able to start to see the goodness, power, and majesty of God, and to restrain them from the kingdom of self—their own self-serving choices. The law to them was grace because it restrained them from evil and pointed them to God.

After wandering in the wilderness forty years because of their rebellion, the Israelites finally came to the Jordan River, the only thing separating them from the promised land and the end of their wandering. They reaffirmed, through Moses, that the Lord would be their God, and the Lord affirmed that the Israelites would be His people (Deut. 26:16–19). They rededicated themselves to the covenant.

In Deuteronomy 27:9–10, Moses told the people, "Take heed and listen, O Israel: This day you have become the people of the LORD your God. Therefore you shall obey the voice of the LORD your God, and observe His commandments and His statutes which I command you today."

Obeying was the first requirement of becoming the people of God. When God made this covenant with Israel, He dictated its words, terms, and conditions. The people agreed and bound themselves to keeping it. The covenant defined the expected behaviors on both sides. The remainder of chapter 27 and all of 28 list the blessings and curses that would come from either keeping or disobeying the law, respectively. The covenantal agreement was an instruction manual in practical godliness—how they should live with each other, how they were to relate to the Lord, and how the Lord would relate to them.

Israel Rejects God and His Law

Despite knowing God, and despite all their promises, the Israelites during the ensuing centuries went through cycles of apostasy. Finally, there came a time after King Solomon died when the Israelites were again self-centered and wouldn't return to God's ways. Solomon's son Rehoboam had succeeded him. Acting on bad advice, he decided to significantly raise taxes on everyone. This so incensed the people that all the tribes of Israel except two renounced their part in the house of David and formed their own kingdom in the north under a new king, Jeroboam. This new northern kingdom was called Israel, and the older southern kingdom was called Judah. The problem was that Jerusalem, and therefore the temple, was in the southern kingdom. King Jeroboam, in order to enforce the separation between the kingdoms and to keep his people from migrating back to Judah, set up a system of worship using idols at the northern and southern borders of his kingdom. He ordered his people to worship the idols and not bother with going to the temple of God in Jerusalem.

Although God continued to send prophets (five in succession) and continually called for Israel to repent and return to their covenant with Him, Israel did not yield. They rejected God's statutes and the covenants they had agreed to, even to the point of no longer believing in the Lord their God (2 Kings 17:14).

Israel rejected God and left Him to follow idols and mix with other nations. Their defection from God was deliberate, open, and irrevocable. Therefore, bound by the rules of the covenant they had made together (to which

God was still faithful while Israel was not), their covenant relationship had to end. Thus, as the prophet Jeremiah describes:

> The LORD said also to me in the days of Josiah the king: "Have you seen what backsliding Israel has done? She has gone up on every high mountain and under every green tree, and there played the harlot. And I said, after she had done all these things, 'Return to Me.' But she did not return. Then I saw that for all the causes for which backsliding Israel had committed adultery, I had put her away and given her a certificate of divorce." (Jer. 3:6–8)

God had tried to woo Israel back to Himself for centuries, but this time she would not come back. So to free her, he gave her a certificate of divorce. He didn't force Israel to stay against her will, and she was not happy to remain with Him. Scripture records that every one of the nineteen kings of Israel "did evil in the sight of the LORD, and walked in the way of Jeroboam, and in his sin by which he had made Israel sin" (1 Kings 15:34).

After Israel was released by God, the country was conquered and its people were carried away captive by the Assyrians. Their downfall is described in 2 Kings 17:19–23. The Assyrians repopulated the land with foreigners from other lands they had conquered, and the captured Israelites were eventually dispersed by the Assyrians as foreigners into other nations as well. Those Israelites have now, for all practical purposes, been lost to history.

God Promises a New Covenant

Even during the process of divorce, God asked Jeremiah (a prophet from Judah) to continue to prophesy to the North. But Jeremiah no longer called to the kingdom as a whole to repent; he now began to call specifically to individuals:

> "Return, O backsliding children," says the LORD; "for I am married to you. I will take you, one from a city and two from a family, and I will bring you to Zion. And I will give you shepherds according to My heart, who will feed you with knowledge and understanding." (Jer. 3:14–15)

God called to those who were backsliding. He assured them that He was still bound and committed to them even if they refused to be married to Him. He would meet them where they were, as children. He promised to cure their backsliding and care for them. The rest of the chapter prophetically talks of a complete restoration, of coming to the city of God in peace and purity, and how, through the tender relationship of a faithful father with his children, it will all happen (Jer. 3:18–19).

Jeremiah goes even further and talks of a future that will include all of us. God wants restoration for us. He wants a relationship with His people that is even better than Adam had in the garden. A new covenant is coming that will be both internal—written on hearts instead of stone—and eternal.

> Behold, the days are coming, says the LORD, when I will make a new covenant with the house of Israel and with the house of Judah— not according to the covenant that I made with their fathers in the day that I took them by the hand to lead them out of the land of Egypt, My covenant which they broke, though I was a husband to them, says the LORD.
>
> But this is the covenant that I will make with the house of Israel after those days," says the LORD: I will put My law in their minds, and write it on their hearts; and I will be their God, and they shall be My people. No more shall every man teach his neighbor, and every man his brother, saying, "Know the LORD," for they all shall know Me, from the least of them to the greatest of them, says the LORD. For I will forgive their iniquity, and their sin I will remember no more. (Jer. 31:31–34)

God's plan has always been our deliverance and restoration. He has always pursued us and has never been unfaithful.

God's Law of Grace and Love

We can see from the examples of the nation of Israel how God, through His grace, restrains our self-destructive inclinations. His goal has always been to remove the very root of our disobedience and sinning, but until then, His laws had two purposes: they exposed sin and provided a defense against it. Even though only one man in all of history ever perfectly kept the law—Christ Jesus—the law was still given as a blessing to Israel.

God's dealings with Israel illustrate the importance of resisting our own instincts and desires (1 Cor. 10:1–14). Their story shows the stark difference in outcomes between following God's directions and following what seemed right to themselves. Over the centuries, God did not vary in His care or concern for His people. He was unwavering in His love and faithful in all His promises. The people, however, wavered among consecration, fall, repentance, reconsecration, coldness, and revival. Peace and prosperity always accompanied their obedience, yet the Israelites consistently drifted back to following their own desires.

God is not a punisher of His people. He is a deliverer. The death sentence on Adam was not from God. Disobedience brings consequences, but God continually directs and encourages His people back to Him and toward actions that lead to life—first wooing them, then sometimes herding them away from the ways of the world that lead to death (Prov. 14:12, 27).

Whenever Israel strayed, God called them back, and the way back always required a rededication to keeping the law as Moses had given it. Whenever Israel responded with repentance, God welcomed them back. These periods of revival always brought prosperity, victory over their enemies, and peace to the nation.

God's law was Israel's schoolmaster, whether written on stone by God's finger or on scrolls by Moses. The requirements of the law kept a consciousness of God foremost in the lives of the Israelites. The precepts were the center of their national identity and distinguished them from other nations. The law restrained the people from being led away by their own desires into sin. It was the mercy and love of God to preserve His people from death and prepare them for the coming of a Savior to remedy the problem of sin itself.

CHAPTER 8

Jesus Brings Understanding

For my eyes have seen Your salvation
Which You have prepared before
the face of all peoples,
A light to bring revelation to the Gentiles,
And the glory of Your people Israel.
Luke 2:30–32

KEY: The things of God appear to be foolishness unless they are spiritually discerned.

Here's our dilemma: No matter how hard we try, no matter what we accomplish, righteousness is out of reach. Our best works only reveal more shortcomings (Rom. 3:20). Therefore, no amount of obedience can bring justification before God, and faith alone is dead. For all have sinned, Jew and gentile. No one is righteous.

We can't escape our consciences because God's law is written deep in the heart of every human (Rom. 2:14–15). But no one can fulfill that law perfectly because our very concept of God was distorted in the garden. Sin is the elephant in the room. I'm not talking about our misdeeds, but about sin itself—the devourer of Cain and the bringer of death.

God had been promising deliverance to Israel for centuries. However, while the religious leaders mistakenly looked for political deliverance, the angel announcing Jesus's advent to Joseph promised spiritual deliverance. Jesus would save people *from* their sins—a much different concept than forgiving people *for* their sins (Matt. 1:20–21). But what is sin?

Sin Is an Internal Brokenness

Hamartia, the Greek word commonly translated as *sin*, is a term from drama that is still used, unchanged, in English. Hamartia, the core dynamic element of a classic tragic play, is an inherent defect or shortcoming in the hero, who in all other respects is a superior being and favored by fortune. It is the tragic character flaw or error in judgment that reverses the protagonist's fortune from good to bad over the course of the play. Common character flaws include excessive ambition, greed, or pride—any of which can result in tragic consequences for the hero.

Most often I have been told that in theology, *hamartia*, and therefore sin, meant to "miss the mark," but I found that to be overly simplistic. Using that definition makes sin easy to explain: God gave a list of rules; if you break a rule, you've missed the mark and haven't met the standard; therefore, it's sin. That may be a logical explanation, but unfortunately, that definition falls short.

Francois du Toit, translator of *The Mirror Bible*, analyzes *hamartia* in this way:

> The word translated sin is the word *hamartia*, from *ha*, negative or without, and *meros*, por-

tion or form; thus to be without your allotted portion or without form: pointing to a disoriented, distorted identity. The word *meros* is the stem of *morphe*, [thus] as used in 2 Corinthians 3:18, the word *metamorphe*, with form, is the opposite of *hamartia*–without form. *Sin is to live out of context with the blueprint of God's design; to behave out of tune with God's original harmony.*[10] (Emphasis added.)

Like the hero in the play, the hamartia—the impediment to glory—must be removed. We can't do it ourselves because we are blind to our own character flaws. The flaw has cracked our core to the point where we don't just need forgiveness and healing; we need a new birth—a do-over from the inside out.

Sin is not just breaking a rule and then becoming subject to punishment from the one who made the rule. That's not the message of Genesis. God directed Adam not to eat of the tree or he would die. God never said He was the one to punish Adam for his disobedience. Rather, something inherent in Adam's decision and act of disobedience immediately changed something *in Adam*. Paul, in Romans, tells us that "through one man sin [hamartia] entered the world, and death through sin, and thus death spread to all men, because all sinned" (Rom. 5:12).

For Adam, sin immediately distorted both his view of God (fear) and of himself (fear and shame). Adam and Eve's eyes were opened, and they saw themselves naked. God didn't open their eyes; sin opened their eyes to their inadequacy and lack. Knowledge of good and evil awakened their consciences to self-condemnation. With God, they had had everything without fear. Now the kingdom of self was born in their hearts, along with fear. Thanks to their newly gained knowledge of good and evil, they could think and judge for themselves, but they found, just as Solomon wrote much later, "There is a way that seems right to a man, but its end is the way of death" (Prov. 14:12).

The Bible tells us that sin entered the world through Adam, and in Adam all died. In this one act, man separated himself from God. He became his own arbiter of truth; his vision was blurred, and his focus was skewed from the truth of God to his own determination of truth. Obedience became optional, and the relationship between Creator and His creation became strained. Man, made in the image of God, remade God in man's own image—a God of his own imagination with flawed passions like his own, easily offended, and meting out justice (punishment) like a man.

The Competing Leadership of the Jews

In Jesus's day, the religious leadership was divided into three main groups. They all believed the law that Moses had received, but not all in the same way. We'll see in a bit how these groups, each acting out of their own self-interest, came together in the condemnation of Jesus.

First, and most influential, were the Pharisees. They believed in the Torah, the written law from Moses. But they also believed those laws were open to interpretation and that God had given Moses the knowledge of what those laws meant and how they should be applied. Those interpretations—the oral law—were codified and written down three centuries after Moses and called the Talmud. Both the Torah and the Talmud were authoritative. The Pharisees valued sophisticated, scholarly interpretation of the Scriptures. They believed in an afterlife and that God punished the wicked and rewarded the righteous in the world to come. They also believed in a messiah who would usher in an era of world peace. They enforced the law on the common people to bring about this peace as soon as possible.

Second were the Sadducees. The Sadducees were elitists who wanted to maintain the priestly caste, but they were also open to incorporating parts of Greek and Roman culture into their lives, which the Pharisees opposed. The Sadducees rejected the oral law and insisted on a literal interpretation of the written law; consequently, they did not believe in an afterlife since it is not mentioned in the Torah. The main focus of Sadducean life was the rituals associated with the temple.

The Essenes, the third faction, emerged out of disgust with the other two. This sect believed the others had corrupted God's holy city, Jerusalem, and the temple. They moved out of Jerusalem and lived a monastic life in the desert, adopting strict dietary laws and a commitment to celibacy.

The Romans occupied Israel and held political and military power. They allowed the Jews to practice their religion, and the Jewish leaders had wide religious authority—as long as they didn't upset the political balance.

The Great Sanhedrin was the Jewish religious supreme court of seventy-one members, made up of Pharisees and Sadducees.

Into this environment came Jesus. The gospel of John opens with His true identity:

> In the beginning [before all time] was the Word (Christ), and the Word was with God, and the Word was God Himself. He was [continually existing] in the beginning [co-eternally] with God. All things were made and came into existence through Him; and without Him not even one thing was made that has come into being. In Him was life [and the power to bestow life], and the life was the Light of men. The Light shines on in the darkness, and the darkness did not understand it or overpower it or appropriate it or absorb it [and is unreceptive to it]. . . .
>
> He (Christ) was in the world, and though the world was made through Him, the world did not recognize Him. He came to that which was His own [that which belonged to Him— His world, His creation, His possession], and those who were His own [people—the Jewish nation] did not receive and welcome Him. But to as many as did receive and welcome Him, He gave the right [the authority, the privilege] to become children of God, that is, to those who believe in (adhere to, trust in, and rely on) His name—who were born, not of blood [natural conception], nor of the will of the flesh [physical impulse], nor of the will of man [that of a natural father], but of God [that is, a divine and supernatural birth—they are born of God—spiritually transformed, renewed, sanctified]. . . .

> For the Law was given through Moses, but grace [the unearned, undeserved favor of God] and truth came through Jesus Christ. No one has seen God [His essence, His divine nature] at any time; the [One and] only begotten God [that is, the unique Son] who is in the intimate presence of the Father, He has explained Him [and interpreted and revealed the awesome wonder of the Father]. (John 1:1–5, 10–13, 17–18 AMP, brackets in the original)

Jesus had been with God eternally and was God. No man had seen God at any time, but to as many as would receive and welcome Him, Jesus came to reveal and explain His Father.

Jesus started His public ministry when He was around thirty years old, introduced openly by John the Baptist, who had announced, "Behold! The Lamb of God who takes away the sin of the world!" (John 1:29). The people considered John to be a prophet (Matt. 21:26), so when John endorsed Jesus and people started following Him, the religious leaders became concerned.

A Puzzled Man Searches for Enlightenment

Nicodemus, a ruler of the Jews, a prominent Pharisee, and a member of the Great Sanhedrin, knew a messiah was coming. Like the other Pharisees, he believed this savior would restore the nation of Israel and deliver them from the current occupation. He was both intrigued and puzzled by Jesus and wanted to talk to Him privately to learn the truth as to who He was and what He was about. We read in John 3 that he came to Jesus by night to question Him. At first it seems as though Jesus gives some strange answers to this Pharisee who is genuinely and humbly looking for truth.

Nicodemus first asks, "Rabbi, we know that You are [at least] a teacher come from God; for no one can do these signs that You do unless God is with him" (John 3:2).

It sounds like a reasonable statement, but Jesus doesn't address it. Jesus replied, "Most assuredly, I say to you, unless one is born again, he cannot see the kingdom of God" (John 3:3).

Nicodemus doesn't take offense at this seeming nonanswer, but he does ask for more explanation. "How can a man be born when he's well past birth age (and size!)? Can he enter again into his mother's womb and redo the trip?" (John 3:4 paraphrased).

Jesus replies again with a longer answer that still doesn't seem to satisfy the question:

> Most assuredly, I say to you, unless one is born of water and the Spirit, he cannot enter the kingdom of God. That which is born of the flesh is flesh, and that which is born of the Spirit is spirit. Do not marvel that I said to you, "You must be born again." (John 3:5–7)

However, on closer examination, we see that Jesus *is* answering the questions Nicodemus poses, but Nicodemus is asking and hearing on a literal level, while Jesus is using natural metaphors to explain spiritual truths. In his opening statement, Nicodemus told Jesus that the miracles he saw proved Jesus was favored by God. Jesus essentially replied, "That's great that you can see that, but unless you're alive in My kingdom, you can't really see where the miracles are coming from."

When asked how in the world it would be possible to be born again physically, Jesus said, "It's not possible in this world, but if you want to see the kingdom of God, you first have to be a human (born of water), but then you also have to be born of the Spirit. Don't be confused. What comes from flesh is flesh. Flesh can only produce flesh, but what is born of the Spirit is spirit. Don't be astounded that I said you have to be born again; you're already aware of things you're not understanding because of your spiritual lack."

Explaining further how the kingdom of God works, Jesus talked about the wind: "The wind blows where it wishes, and you hear the sound of it, but cannot tell where it comes from and where it goes. So is everyone who is born of the Spirit" (John 3:8). Thus, just as Nicodemus had seen Jesus's miracles, yet didn't understand where they came from, so is the wind. It comes and we see its effects, but we can't see the impetus behind it. You don't know where it came from or where it's going next. Everyone born of the Spirit is the same. Each one carries an energy and purpose unknown to the natural observer.

Nicodemus was befuddled and still had trouble grasping what Jesus was saying: "How can these things be?" (John 3:9).

Jesus, seemingly in amazement and slightly reproachful, said, "Are you the teacher of Israel, and do not know these things?" (John 3:10).

This is the blindness I've been talking about. Nicodemus was a spiritual leader, a Pharisee of God's own set-apart, holy nation. He was recognized and represented himself as an expert in spiritual things, especially those things outlined in God's law. Yet Jesus exposed the fact that he couldn't see spiritually. He couldn't see the kingdom of God and didn't understand even the most basic principles of how things worked there.

Jesus took Nicodemus's exclamation of "How can these things be?" as unbelief. Nicodemus had studied the Scriptures and was listening to an eyewitness, yet he still had trouble believing.

> Most assuredly, I say to you, We speak what We know and testify what We have seen, and you do not receive Our witness. If I have told you earthly things and you do not believe, how will you believe if I tell you heavenly things? No one has ascended to heaven but He who came down from heaven, that is, the Son of Man who is in heaven. (John 3:11–13)

Jesus had been in heaven and came down from heaven. Therefore, Nicodemus should have been able to believe Him when He talked about heavenly things. But who is the "We" in this passage who know and have seen? I believe the answer is in John 8:38, where Jesus said, "I speak what I have seen with my father." What had Jesus seen with His Father that fits into this discussion with Nicodemus? Psalm 14:2 may have the answer: "The LORD looks down from heaven upon the children of men, to see if there are any who understand, who seek God." None were found. But the psalm ends with a cry for the salvation of Israel to come out of Zion to release God's people from captivity, specifically the captivity of not knowing God (Ps. 14:1–4).

That Savior was sitting there with Nicodemus, opening his eyes to the truth. When Jesus told the Pharisee that He had come from heaven, He had just told him who He was.

We know Nicodemus eventually understood these answers and believed, since he is mentioned later in John's gospel as providing the spices and assisting Joseph of Arimathea in preparing the body of Jesus for burial, a task they had to do secretly for fear of the Jewish leaders (John 19:38–42).

The Simile of the Serpent

Next, Jesus moved on from telling Nicodemus who He was and began to tell him what He was about, His future, and His mission.

> And as Moses lifted up the serpent in the wilderness, even so must the Son of Man be lifted up, that whoever believes in Him should not perish but have eternal life. For God so loved the world that He gave His only begotten Son, that whoever believes in Him should not perish but have everlasting life. For God did not send His Son into the world to condemn the world, but that the world through Him might be saved. (John 3:14–17)

How was the serpent in the wilderness lifted up? It was

lifted up on a pole for all to see, just as Jesus would be physically lifted up on the cross. But that physical viewing alone was not enough to cause belief. Jesus, just as He has been doing for this whole discussion, is speaking from a spiritual perspective, not physical. This has deeper meaning. The story of the serpent is told in Numbers 21. The Israelites had been wandering in the wilderness, following Moses, for almost forty years. Once again, with the promised land almost in sight, Moses seemed to be leading them in a different direction, and the people became very discouraged.

> And the people spoke against God and against Moses: "Why have you brought us up out of Egypt to die in the wilderness? For there is no food and no water, and our soul loathes this worthless bread." So the LORD sent fiery serpents among the people, and they bit the people; and many of the people of Israel died.
>
> Therefore the people came to Moses, and said, "We have sinned, for we have spoken against the LORD and against you; pray to the LORD that He take away the serpents from us." So Moses prayed for the people.
>
> Then the LORD said to Moses, "Make a fiery serpent, and set it on a pole; and it shall be that everyone who is bitten, when he looks at it, shall live." So Moses made a bronze serpent, and put it on a pole; and so it was, if a serpent had bitten anyone, when he looked at the bronze serpent, he lived. (Num. 21:5–9)

These were God's chosen people, the Israelites, grumbling against God and His representative, Moses. They were telling God that His plans for them were not good—in fact, they believed His plans were for their deaths! They attributed the fruit of sin—death—to the plans of God, thereby calling God evil. How appropriate that the very symbol of deception and death came immediately in great numbers to destroy them! They had rejected God, from whom all life comes. They rejected His leadership and provision, and were experiencing the consequences. "Fiery serpents" are poisonous snakes, and just as sin poisons the soul, their poison spread through the body and brought death.

The people repented. They said to Moses, "We have sinned; intervene on our behalf." At this point, their words alone were not enough. There had to be evidence of faith, and faith without action is a dead faith (James 1:22; 2:26). The Israelites couldn't promise that from then on they would be good—because they wouldn't. They couldn't. But they could believe God would allow them to come to Him by faith—even by Moses's faith.

God made a way—only one way. They were to look at the bronze serpent that Moses had made, and they were to look on it in faith. The word for *looked* in Numbers 21:9 means to "look expectantly or intensely." The people had a choice. If they looked—putting action to their faith—they would live. If they didn't look, they would die. The people had to look intently on the consequences of their sin. A glance wasn't enough. Their sin was not the serpent on the pole. Their sin was complaining against both God and Moses and calling what was good, evil. The consequence of their sin was the poisonous serpents. There was no way of salvation other than saying, "We have sinned, and we will die unless God saves us." They had no answer in themselves, and checking their latest survival manual was useless. But they believed in God and in Moses and in the way of escape provided, and they were healed.

Jesus continued telling Nicodemus that He, the Son of Man, must be lifted up, just as the serpent in the wilderness had been lifted up. The implication here is that the snakes were already among the people, and the poison from their sin was already spreading!

The bronze serpent on the pole was harmless in itself, but it was the image of the poisonous beast that was bringing death to the people. Those serpents had been called and empowered by the people's rebellion. Long ago, Adam and Eve had chosen their own way instead of God's and had suffered and died because of a single serpent. Now, in the wilderness, innumerable serpents were biting and killing the people. But God was their faithful savior, just as He said in Isaiah: "When the enemy comes in like a flood, the Spirit of the LORD will lift up a standard against him. 'The Redeemer will come to Zion, and to those who turn from transgression in Jacob'" (Is. 59:19–20).

That wilderness pole for us is Jesus's cross of crucifixion (John 12:31–33). It is God's standard raised up against sin and all its effects. Whoever acknowledges that he has already been poisoned by sin, confesses his rebellion, and looks expectantly at the cross, trusting in God's provision for salvation, will be saved.

Just as one earnest gaze done in faith—no matter how

weak—at the serpent on the pole brought an instantaneous cure to their bodies, so real faith in the Lord Jesus, no matter how feeble, will bring certain and instantaneous healing to the spiritually perishing. However, as Jesus stresses to Nicodemus, the condemnation of not obeying is the same in both scenarios (John 3:18).

The apostle Paul later elaborates on these two analogies of Jesus: being born again of the Spirit, and the physical image of sin becoming God's way of deliverance:

> The law of the Spirit of life in Christ Jesus has made me free from the law of sin and death. For what the law could not do in that it was weak through the flesh, God did by sending His own Son in the likeness of sinful flesh, on account of sin: He condemned sin in the flesh, that the righteous requirement of the law might be fulfilled in us who do not walk according to the flesh but according to the Spirit. (Rom. 8:2–4)

This message of the cross "is foolishness to those who are perishing, but to us who are being saved it is the power of God" (1 Cor. 1:18). We overthink and miss the point. As one commentator points out:

> Doubtless many bitten Israelites, galling as their case was, would *reason* rather than *obey,* would *speculate* on the absurdity of expecting the bite of a living serpent to be cured by looking at a piece of lifeless metal in the shape of one—speculate thus *till they died.* Alas! is not

> salvation by a crucified Redeemer subjected to
> like treatment? Has the 'offense of the cross' yet
> ceased?[11]

The cross of Christ is an offense to the proud. However, when I look away from myself and gaze intently at the bloodied body of Jesus on the cross and say, "I helped put Him there; *that* is what my sin really looks like: *that* is what my sin brings into existence," my pretense of self-righteousness drops away. To embrace this is to humble myself before God; it is the last surrender and the death of the ego. But it is also the narrow way that leads to life and freedom.

A New View of the Conquering Messiah

Jewish religious leaders of this time were looking for a messiah who would deliver Israel from all its oppressors and lead them into a glorious new age. He was to be a conquering messiah. There were also strong suggestions, especially from the Psalms and prophets, that he would be free from sin, perform at least some priestly duties, and suffer.

But Jesus was telling Nicodemus that God didn't send His Son into the world to condemn it or purge it of unrighteous people, but God purposed to save the world through the Son (John 3:16–17). It was to be through Jesus's death—receiving, in His innocence, the wages of sin—that death would be conquered and sin would be made powerless. "For He made Him who knew no sin to be sin for us, that we might become the righteousness of God in Him" (2 Cor. 5:21).

Jesus reiterated that whoever believes in—entrusts

themselves to—Him is not condemned, because He is the Savior. Because of sin, the default position of man is condemnation to death (John 3:18). However, God is not the one doing the condemning. He is providing the way out, through Jesus, to men who are condemned already! The image of the bronze serpent on a pole still applies to this part of Jesus's declaration. If one turns with faith, there is salvation. If one does not turn, he remains condemned to die, overcome by the virulence and corruption of sin.

This is the basis for any judgment against us: the light has come into the world, and people have a clear choice. The light shines on all, and light exposes. Evildoers love the darkness and avoid the light because if they come to the light, their deeds will be exposed and they will be condemned. In contrast, those people who *do* the truth come to the light willingly, unafraid of their deeds being exposed because the light will show that they were done by God's empowerment and in dependence on Him. Because God is truth, the deeds He prompts and empowers are also true and therefore righteous (John 3:19–21).

We can't be saved by our works, but our faith can be judged by our works.

CHAPTER 9

The End of Condemnation

There is therefore now no condemnation to those who are in Christ Jesus, who do not walk according to the flesh, but according to the Spirit. For the law of the Spirit of life in Christ Jesus has made me free from the law of sin and death.
Romans 8:1–2

KEY: The humble are saved and comforted by the justice and order of the kingdom of God.

Jesus came to take away the sin of the world—to, with finality, deal with sin and all its effects. During His ministry, much to the horror of the Pharisees, Jesus not only forgave individuals' sins, but also demonstrated His authority to mend the *effects* of sin in this world by physically healing people and doing other miracles (1 John 3:5–8). He received this authority from His Father (John 5:19–30).

The Bible teaches that sin is the core problem. Our individual sins are only the symptoms that prove the disease (sin) is there. Are our sins still damaging us? Do they need to be dealt with? Do we need to be cleansed from them and their effects? Absolutely yes! The little foxes spoil the vines

(Song 2:15), a little leaven can leaven the whole lump (1 Cor. 5:6), and one fly in the ointment can ruin the whole pot (Eccl. 10:1). We are to deal with our individual sins (1 John 1:8–10). In the Old Testament, God provided a way for forgiveness through acts of obedience and commitment to Him. The sacrificial system was God's vehicle of grace to His people. Now Jesus has brought a better way.

Since early Sunday school, I was taught that Jesus was sent to earth to die because my sins needed forgiving before I could stand unashamed before God and go to heaven. I needed to acknowledge that He had died for me personally, and I had to accept His offer to pay the debt that my sins had incurred with God. In other words, I deserved punishment from God for my deeds, but Jesus had graciously and mercifully taken my punishment, thus paying my debt so I could go free and go to heaven. I followed the directions of Romans 10:9–10: I confessed with my mouth that Jesus was my Lord and believed in my heart that God had raised Him from the dead. So, I should be saved. But there was a certain uneasiness. When I was honest with myself, I had to admit I wasn't feeling love for God. Sometimes I had flashes of it, but most often it was absent, and I was left with just duty. I knew I *should* love Him. I mean, how much more could I ask Him to do for me than die for me? But duty never births love. You can never genuinely love someone only out of obligation.

An Inadequate Redemption

My problem was the model of salvation I had been taught was wrong. In my spiritual instruction, the process of salvation looked like this: God the Father sits as a court-room judge ready to pass sentence on me. I am unargu-ably guilty. The judge declares my sentence: it is death—a righteous and well-deserved sentence because the Bible says that the soul that sins will die (Ezek. 18:20) and that the wages of sin is death (Rom. 6:23). I've definitely sinned against God, and now the penalty is due. But suddenly, Jesus Himself stands up and says, "Let the sentence fall on me! I love this man, and I ask permission to take his pen-alty." The judge agrees because justice demands the sentence be carried out. Strangely, in this scenario the carrying out of the sentence is somehow more important than on whom the judgment falls. In this system it makes no difference whether I suffer the penalty or Jesus suffers the penalty. Justice is lowered to become only a merciless mechanism demanding satisfaction.

At first this sounds like good news. I get to go free with no more than a heartfelt thank-you to Jesus. However, as I sat meditating one day on that scene and visualizing my walking through it, I realized that if it happened that way, I would feel worse! My guilt and bondage would *increase*, not decrease. Yes, I would walk free of my death sentence, but I would know that an innocent man, one who loved me, had died in my place. I would be free outside, but not inside. I wouldn't feel or believe I was truly cleansed from my sins. Instead, it would feel like one more had been added! That process may be legal, but it doesn't feel like justice; it feels more like I beat the system through a legal loophole that the judge somehow allowed because he was running the system. I knew I would still cringe in guilt if

I ever met the judge again, even outside the courtroom, because we would both still know the truth of what I was.

In my church, I was told I should just believe that I had been declared no longer guilty. If I had feelings to the contrary, I should resist them and even deny them. If I had feelings of doubt, it was because I didn't have faith in God's—the judge's—Word and needed more teaching about it. I knew I needed more assurance. Maybe I needed to go forward and surrender my life again in rededication.

The superficiality of that scenario was the cause of my discomfort. The explanation was deficient because it only explained the forgiveness of my sins by the payment of my debt. It couldn't explain the internal cleansing work of God that I needed on my conscience. Our consciences have condemned us ever since they learned the knowledge of good and evil. Adam's conscience drove him into hiding in the garden, and we've been only tentatively coming out ever since. We've been afraid of total exposure. We've done everything to avoid nakedness. We've been afraid of the Light.

Cleansing our Conscience

God, through His righteousness, cleanses our consciences of guilt and condemnation. Hebrews chapter 10 explains that Christ's cleansing work is so complete that we are freed from even the awareness of sin.

In Jesus's work of atonement, the fear and self-consciousness we had before God is dissolved. Our consciences are cleansed, and a new boldness arises. This is much more than getting off on a legal technicality. It's much better than just being forgiven. God, through Jesus, triumphs and changes us at our core. The truth is so much better than most of us have been told. What Adam lost, God restored. We not only gained righteousness, but also forgiveness of and release from sin itself. We experience new life as God's adopted children. Jesus came to completely destroy the works of the devil that were meant to keep us bound in sin (1 John 3:7–10).

God has never been willing that any should perish. He has been exceedingly patient with mankind, wooing us back to Himself and leading us to repentance (2 Peter 3:9). Throughout human history, man has always left God; God never left man.

What about the Wrath of God?

Man has always had a choice: follow God's laws and find life, or follow what seems right to him (his own law) and find death. God has not judged man—in fact, He has actively restrained Himself and delayed judgment. As Peter says, "Consider that the longsuffering of our Lord is salvation" (2 Peter 3:15). It is the goodness of God that leads us to repentance (Rom. 2:4). Thus, in a sense, what we perceive as the "wrath of God" is His leaving us to experience the consequences of our own choices.

However, mercy is not license. There will be a time of settling accounts and a time for avenging wrongs done (Rev. 6:9–11). The discussion of those details is beyond the scope of this book, but know that God's wrath is not the problem, but the solution. It is the long-awaited vindication of justice after the tension of the prophets' "O LORD, how long shall I cry . . .?" (Hab. 1:2).

We take heart in knowing there is no need for us to ever

be part of the condemned. Rather, those who are redeemed and committed to God are part of His divine rescue plan for the world as our works and witness point people to God's salvation (Matt. 5:16). As Peter assures us, "Beloved, do not forget this one thing, . . . the Lord is . . . longsuffering toward us, not willing that any should perish but that all should come to repentance" (2 Peter 3:8–9).

To Reach Mankind, God Came Down

God is good, compassionate, and merciful to us. But what can He do with people who are blind? What does He do with people who are "given over"? What does He do with those people who are consumed with "justice" and "fairness" and are convinced that it is only their definition of justice that is correct? They don't see that their own judgment of right and wrong, of what is good and evil, is at odds with God's definition.

For God, *justice* means to set things right—to restore things to how He meant them to be. God never abandoned His creation, but continually calls men and women back to relationship with Him. In contrast, most people—even many believers—believe justice means retribution and punishment. Driven by both jealousy and inadequacy, we often try in vain to "make things even."

To save us, God had to get dirty. In the form of Jesus, God was born as a man. The Creator became a creature; the last Adam (Jesus) was born into this world as a dust-of-the-ground human. He lived life as a man, dependent on His Father in heaven.

Jesus's descent into humility occurred in three steps:

1. Jesus emptied Himself of His glory (Phil. 2:5–8).

As a man, Jesus lived a life of obedience, subject to His Father, even obeying to the extent of dying. He died an unimaginably painful and shameful death as He hung on the cross naked. Further, to the Jews, anyone who had been hung on a tree was cursed and was placed outside of God's covenant people (Deut. 21:23; Gal. 3:13).

2. He took on our humanity. Immortality put on mortality.
3. He lived as a slave rather than as Lord of all.

Jesus as a Slave

Jesus took "the form of a bondservant" (Phil. 2:7). The word *bondservant* is from the Greek *doulos*, which means "a slave, one who is in permanent relation of servitude to another, his will being altogether consumed in the will of the other (Matt. 8:9; 20:27; 24:45–46). Generally, one serving, bound to serve, in bondage" (Rom. 6:16–17).[12]

To whom was Jesus a bondservant? Certainly, as God, He couldn't be a slave to Himself.

The answer is twofold. Jesus emptied Himself and left His position of glory. Thus, it was in His humanity that He fully submitted to His Father. This is clear in John chapter 17 when Jesus says in His prayer to His Father, "I have finished the work which You have given Me to do."

Jesus was altogether consumed in the will of His Father: "Though He was a Son, yet He learned obedience by the things which He suffered. And having been perfected,

He became the author of eternal salvation to all who obey Him" (Heb. 5:8–9).

In His humanity, Jesus was one with His Father through His obedience, just as salvation comes to all people through their belief in and obedience to Jesus (John 5:19, 24; 8:28–29). The word *believe* means to entrust ourselves to Him.

But Jesus also, in concert with the will of His Father and in full obedience to Him, became a servant to *us*, to humankind. "For even the Son of Man did not come to be served, but to serve, and to give His life a ransom for many" (Mark 10:45).

On the night of the Last Supper, Jesus emphasized this point, to Peter's bewilderment, by washing the feet of the disciples. At the very point where Jesus saw victory, when His finish line was in sight, and when He knew He would soon be returning to the Father, He served.

> Then He came to Simon Peter. And Peter said to Him, "Lord, are You washing my feet?"
>
> Jesus answered and said to him, "What I am doing you do not understand now, but you will know after this."
>
> Peter said to Him, "You shall never wash my feet!"
>
> Jesus answered him, "If I do not wash you, you have no part with Me." (John 13:6–8)

It wasn't until after Jesus's death that Peter understood (2 Peter 1:1).

CHAPTER 10

Two Kingdoms, Two Words, and Reconciliation

And you, who once were alienated and enemies
in your mind by wicked works, yet now He has
reconciled in the body of His flesh through death,
to present you holy, and blameless, and above
reproach in His sight.
Colossians 1:21–22

KEY: Jesus's work of reconciliation breaks down humankind's wall of separation between themselves and God.

From Adam onward through history, man consistently chose his own way. The fruit of the Tree of the Knowledge of Good and Evil solidified man's belief that his ways and opinions were righteous and just, while God was a self-centered taskmaster with rules that made life harder. As humankind lost its clear vision of God, it depended more and more on its own understanding of what it believed God *should* be like. Pleasing that god depended on keeping the rules—because having a personal relationship like Abraham, Moses, or David had seemed out of reach.

This pattern of self-reliance and the belief that keeping rules well was the path to God continued through the Old Testament right up through the Pharisees of Jesus's day. Those Jewish religious leaders substituted empty obedience for the true worship of God. Outwardly they kept the rules very well, but in their hearts they had lost the image of HaShem Elohim, the loving Father behind the law. They gave lip service to God's commandments and rulership, but they had changed and added to those commands in an attempt to please a god that thought and acted like them. They weren't serving God; they were running their own religious kingdom based on their own impaired understanding.

As Jesus said to them:

> Hypocrites! Well did Isaiah prophesy about you, saying:
> "These people draw near to Me with their mouth,
> And honor Me with their lips,
> But their heart is far from Me.
> And in vain they worship Me,
> Teaching as doctrines the commandments of men." (Matt. 15:7–9)

"In vain they worship Me." Why in vain? Not because God was unresponsive, but because they were worshiping a god of their own making and in their own image: a god that acted like themselves. They were keeping lots of rules, but they weren't obeying *God*.

Two Kingdoms in Conflict

This is still the problem today. Each individual wants his own kingdom: a kingdom of self. The king of this kingdom is always confident, self-focused, demanding, and entitled. He is quick to criticize, quick to judge, quick to put others down, and quick to condemn because people are always violating the laws of his kingdom. The greatest moral offense in the king's life is people's disobedience of the laws of his kingdom. He is both self-righteous and easily offended.

Humans were created to live in intimacy and dependency on God for life and happiness. Our tendency, however, especially as adults, is to avoid God. We do not want the light of God's judgment to shine into our carefully ordered kingdoms. A separation of our own making has been fixed between God and humans—placed there mostly unconsciously—because we don't want to yield kingship to God. We have determined that His ways are unjust.

The disconnection is between two kingdoms: the kingdom of self and the kingdom of God. Both have a king and both have laws, but death reigns in one and life in the other. The kingdom of self has been at enmity with God since the garden.

> For those who live according to the flesh set their minds on the things of the flesh, but those who live according to the Spirit, the things of the Spirit. For to be carnally minded is death, but to be spiritually minded is life and peace. Because the carnal mind is enmity against God;

> for it is not subject to the law of God, nor in-
> deed can be. So then, those who are in the flesh
> cannot please God. (Rom. 8:5–8)

The carnal mind rules the kingdom of self. It cannot please God, despite its best efforts to be righteous. Even keeping the law, if it's done only as obeying a set of rules, is not acceptable. This kingdom, in its self-centeredness, is offended by true righteousness (Gen. 4:5–7).

> Therefore by the deeds of the law no flesh will
> be justified in His sight, for by the law is the
> knowledge of sin. But now the righteousness
> of God apart from the law is revealed, being
> witnessed by the Law and the Prophets, even
> the righteousness of God through faith in Jesus
> Christ, to all and on all who believe.
>
> For there is no difference; for all have sinned
> and fall short of the glory of God, being justi-
> fied freely by His grace through the redemption
> that is in Christ Jesus, whom God set forth as
> a propitiation by His blood, through faith, to
> demonstrate His righteousness, because in His
> forbearance God had passed over the sins that
> were previously committed, to demonstrate at
> the present time His righteousness, that He
> might be just and the justifier of the one who
> has faith in Jesus. (Rom. 3:20–26)

The law cannot bring about salvation from sin because the law's purpose is to reveal sin. But through faith in Jesus, a righteousness unconstrained by the law is revealed—not just forgiveness, but a righteousness that can cleanse and satisfy consciences. All have sinned, and all have been justified freely by God's grace through the redemption that is in Christ Jesus, whom God sent as a propitiation by His blood. The law is powerless to justify, but the way of salvation is open to us all by grace.

And here is the glory, where we start to see a glimpse of the scope of the compassionate wisdom and justice woven throughout God's plan of redemption. Jesus was sent to die, but His death wasn't only to satisfy God's wrath, although it did both demonstrate and satisfy God's righteousness and justice. Jesus was sent as a *propitiation*. And that leads us to look carefully at two particular words.

Important Words, Lost in Greek

Orge

What is the wrath of God? From our vantage point in the twenty-first century, we don't always understand the English words in older Bible translations the same way as the seventeenth-century translators intended. For example, the word translated consistently through the book of Romans as *wrath* is the Greek word *orge*. Overall, *orge* appears thirty-six times in the New Testament manuscripts from which the King James Bible was translated. The translators rendered it with various English words, depending on the context. It's translated "wrath" thirty-one times, "anger" three times, and once each as "vengeance" and "indignation."

Adding to our difficulty in understanding, the common usage of the word *wrath* has changed over the years.

Today, *wrath* connotes violent, intense anger, but in the Greek when that type of violent anger was indicated, they used an entirely different word, *thymos,* which means a hot anger, an anger boiling up in passion. *Thymos* is used in Luke 4:28, Acts 19:28, Revelation 12:12, and other passages.

In contrast, the word *orge* refers to an ongoing indignation. It can be translated as "anger," but it refers to the type of anger exhibited after deliberation, as in a deserved punishment, specifically of punishments inflicted by magistrates. Webster's *American Dictionary of the English Language* of 1828 gives a closer rendering of the word as it was understood at the time of the King James translation in 1611: "The effects of anger" or "the just punishment of an offense or crime."[13] It can also mean the punishment itself, as in Romans 8:1, where it is translated as "condemnation."

God's wrath, in Scripture, is His holy and just indignation against sin. It does not describe cold, heartless vengeance for an offense, but well-considered consequences meted out under law.

Hilasterion

Hilasterion is the Greek word that is variously translated as "propitiation" or "expiation," depending on the context.

Propitiation is "the act of appeasing wrath and conciliating the favor of an offended person; the act of making propitious."[14]

Expiation is the alternate definition of *hilasterion*, and means

> The act of atoning for a crime; the act of making satisfaction for an offense, by which the guilt is done away, and the obligation of the offended person to punish the crime is canceled; atonement; satisfaction.
>
> Among pagans and Jews, expiation was made chiefly by sacrifices, or washings and purification. Among Christians, expiation for the sins of men is usually considered as made only by the obedience and sufferings of Christ.[15]

Both words are correct in their own way because there is a tension between the meanings. If there's too much emphasis on expiation, it appears God is only concerned with the legalities of the offense. In other words, Jesus merely covered sin, paid the penalty, and our legal debt was settled. Conversely, too much emphasis on propitiation makes it look like God is a tyrant who needs to be mollified, and Jesus merely appeased God's holy anger. Either view, if taken alone, is contrary to God's character of righteousness and justice.

In one other place, *hilasterion* is translated differently. In Hebrews 9:5 it means "mercy seat" and refers to the cover of the ark of the covenant in the tabernacle, the place of mercy and meeting (Ex. 25:22; Lev. 16). In the Old Testament, the high priest atoned for Israel's sins by sprinkling blood on the lid of the ark and making confession for the sins of the people.

Romans tells us that, in the middle of mankind's universal sinfulness, God offers justification to all by His grace.

Christ is the propitiation, offered by God to all mankind, to be received by faith. All men have sinned, and the wages of sin (singular, not plural) is death, "but the gift of God is eternal life in [*through*] Jesus Christ our Lord" (Rom. 3:23; 6:23). His blood—that is, His life—spilled out in His death, provides that promised gift of life to all who will receive it.

The Triumph of Reconciliation

The idea Paul expresses is not that of an angry God who needs to be conciliated, but an expiation of sin by a merciful God through the atoning death of His Son. It in no way excludes the reality of God's righteous wrath because of sin. However, God is much less concerned with individual trespasses than He is with the corruption of sin that led to those choices. God has always hated sin and what it does to His creation.

The wages of sin is death. The end of sin is death (Rom. 6:23; James 1:15). Christ is, therefore, the means of satisfaction for sin. His blood is efficacious for our salvation because it is the evidence of His life sacrificed in atonement (Gen. 9:4; Lev. 17:11; Deut. 12:23).

Our justification on these grounds has nothing to do with our moral merit or spiritual effort. It comes to us by God's grace as a gift. In other words, we are acquitted for nothing, without price, only out of the undeserved, unearned love of God. Because of this once-for-all method of dealing with sin, people's sins in the past were temporarily overlooked (the forbearance of God). The penalty for sins in the present is also delayed. God can do all this with perfect righteousness since He is both just and the justifier of those who believe in or entrust themselves to Jesus (Rom. 3:21–26).

We can easily see Jesus's death as a propitiatory offering to God. His offering both satisfies sin's demand for death and confirms God's righteous justice, for God is the one who both requires and supplies the sacrifice (Gen. 22:7–8).

But the startling realization for me was that Christ's propitiation didn't go only one way. Look again at this passage: "Christ Jesus, whom God set forth as a propitiation by His blood, through faith" (Rom. 3:24–25). God set forth Jesus as a propitiation—but God isn't the one who needed to receive a propitiation by faith. We did!

"God demonstrates His own love toward us, in that while we were still sinners, Christ died for us" (Rom. 5:8).

We were all ruling over our own kingdoms of self when God *came to us*, in the flesh, as one of us. He offered Himself as a propitiation to us, acknowledging our blindness and our own pseudo-kingdoms, and allowed us to judge and sentence Him out of our self-created and perverted sense of justice.

We, even while we were still deceived in our sin, were allowed to judge and sentence God.

God offered Himself, in Jesus, as a propitiation to us! He is an offering of peace and reconciliation in a war of our own making that we don't even realize we are in! None of the evil we've experienced is from God. All His plans for us are good. He is not scheming to catch us or to condemn us. We are already condemned (John 3:17–21). He's looking to save those who will trust Him. "For the eyes of the

LORD run to and fro throughout the whole earth, to show Himself strong on behalf of those whose heart is loyal to Him" (2 Chron. 16:9).

What a mystery! This is the gospel. God sent His Son into the world, not to condemn the world, "but that the world through Him might be saved" (John 3:17). God, in Jesus, came to us and submitted to mankind as a servant. He became fully human.

At the same time, Jesus, as a man, submitted Himself to God and broke the power of sin and death, thus reconciling all mankind to God. God, in Jesus, reconciled the world to Himself, not Himself to the world (2 Cor. 5:19). He died so that we who live could stop living for ourselves, but instead, live for Him and in Him (2 Cor. 5:15). Through Him we are both reconciled to and made one with God (John 17:21–23). He closed the man-made gulf between us, and as we'll see in coming chapters, through His blood on the mercy seat of heaven, He reopened the place of face-to-face meeting between God and man.

CHAPTER 11

The End of an Age

*For there is one God and one Mediator between
God and men, the Man Christ Jesus, who gave
Himself a ransom for all, to be testified in
due time.*
1 Timothy 2:5–6

KEY: The old is annulled, and the new is coming: Jesus is the Mediator of a better covenant.

God came to us. He has always come to us. However, when the Creator of the universe came to this world in human flesh, His own creatures failed to recognize Him. "He came to His own, and His own did not receive Him" (John 1:11). In other words, He came specifically to His own covenant people, and His people, who claimed loyalty to Him, didn't know Him.

He came to woo His people back, showing them the true heart of His Father, which was also His own. Jesus didn't come brandishing His rights as a king; He came serving (Mark 10:45). He called for His people to repent, leave their little kingdoms, and return to live in His kingdom again. He called to all those who were dead in their trespasses and sins to trust Him, believe in Him, and give up their illusion of life through their dead works. He called us to come back to Life Himself. He came to reshow us His Father, who, to as many as love Jesus and keep His commandments, becomes "our Father" (John 14:23–24).

However, in the hearts of the very people who should have recognized and acclaimed the coming of God—the Pharisees, Sadducees, scribes, chief priests, and elders—Jesus provoked indignation. Conversely, many of the Jewish common people believed on Him because of His teachings and miracles (John 11:45). He mixed with the common people and offended the sophisticated.

After one especially impressive miracle, raising His friend Lazarus from the dead, the chief priests and Pharisees gathered in a council and said, "What shall we do? For this Man works many signs. If we let Him alone like this, everyone will believe in Him, and the Romans will come and take away both our place and nation" (John 11:47–48). These religious officials were not concerned about knowing the truth and being faithful representatives of God; they were concerned only about their position.

The council concluded, "It is expedient for us that one man should die for the people, and not that the whole nation should perish" (John 11:50). And "from that day on, they plotted to put [Jesus] to death" (John 11:53).

The Trial of Jesus

The council's opportunity came when one of Jesus's disciples, Judas, came to the leaders offering to betray Jesus for money. Not many days later, during the Jewish Passover Feast, he was able to do so and delivered Jesus to a contingent of Roman soldiers sent by the Jewish leaders to bring

Jesus back for preliminary trial before the high priest and the council of elders and scribes.

When Jesus stood before the full Sanhedrin in formal trial, they found Him guilty of blasphemy and worthy of death (Matt. 26:65–66). Thus, the Jewish religious leaders passed their united judgment on Jesus, the Son of God, and plotted His death. Blasphemy was their excuse; saving their own status within the Roman administration was their reason.[16]

The Sanhedrin could condemn Jesus to death, but they couldn't carry out the execution. They were in occupied Roman territory and were bound by Roman governance. Capital punishment was the province of the Romans; therefore, the Jewish leaders had to scheme how to have Jesus put to death when He hadn't broken any Roman laws.

They bound Jesus and took Him to Pontius Pilate, the Roman governor. They brought many charges, but only one seems to have held any significance to Pilate: He needed to determine whether Jesus was a king and whether there was any threat to Rome.

> Pilate then went out to them and said, "What accusation do you bring against this Man?"
>
> They answered and said to him, "If He were not an evildoer, we would not have delivered Him up to you."
>
> Then Pilate said to them, "You take Him and judge Him according to your law."
>
> Therefore the Jews said to him, "It is not lawful for us to put anyone to death," that the saying of Jesus might be fulfilled which He spoke, signifying by what death He would die.

> Then Pilate entered the Praetorium again, called Jesus, and said to Him, "Are You the King of the Jews?"
>
> Jesus answered him, "Are you speaking for yourself about this, or did others tell you this concerning Me?"
>
> Pilate answered, "Am I a Jew? Your own nation and the chief priests have delivered You to me. What have You done?" (John 18:29–35)

Pilate found no fault in Jesus, but when he told his findings to the chief priests and the Jews, they were even more enraged. They wouldn't be pacified. They said, "He stirs up the people, teaching throughout all Judea, beginning from Galilee to this place" (Luke 23:5). Galilee! This gave Pilate the opportunity he needed to try to rid himself of all these demanding people in his Praetorium (judgment hall). Herod Antipas, whom the Romans had appointed native ruler of Galilee, was in Jerusalem, and Galilee was his territory! So Pilate sent Jesus, along with the crowd, to Herod.

Herod had long wanted to see Jesus and because of His reputation, was hoping to see Jesus, perform some miracle. But Jesus answered none of his questions. Herod, offended and frustrated, mocked Jesus, abused Him, then gave Him a kingly robe and sent Him back to Pilate (Luke 23:6–12).

Pilate was exasperated by the whole situation. Neither he nor Herod had found any fault in Jesus. Then Pilate practically accused the Jews of stirring up trouble through their stubborn, but baseless, accusations against Jesus:

You have brought this Man to me, as one who
misleads the people. And indeed, having exam-
ined Him in your presence, I have found no
fault in this Man concerning those things of
which you accuse Him; no, neither did Herod,
for I sent you back to him; and indeed nothing deserving of death has been done by Him.
(Luke 23:14–15)

Pilate had only one other option if he were to avoid
a riot. The city was packed because of Passover. If he allowed mob rule, he might be found unfit to govern and
would lose his position—the same fear troubling the Jewish leaders. He knew that Jesus was innocent and had been
brought before him only because of those leaders' envy
(Matt. 27:18). He had only one more tactic he could try to
both save an innocent man and preserve the peace.

At the feast, Pilate had the custom of releasing one
prisoner, whom the people could choose. He proposed to
release either a reprehensible criminal named Barabbas, or
Jesus. The choice was clear. "But the chief priests stirred
up the crowd, so that he should rather release Barabbas to
them" (Mark 15:11).

The description we are given of Barabbas is uncannily
like that of Jesus's description to the Pharisees in John 10:10
of the thief who comes to steal the sheep and bypasses the
door. He said, "The thief does not come except to steal, and
to kill, and to destroy." The leaders of the Jews were leading the people astray. They were deliberately steering God's
people away from proper justice—and away from God.
They chose to free Barabbas instead of Jesus. Barabbas was

a robber (John 18:40), an insurrectionist, and a murderer (Luke 23:19). He was a thief, a destroyer, and a killer.

> So then Pilate took Jesus and scourged Him. And the soldiers twisted a crown of thorns and put it on His head, and they put on Him a purple robe. Then they said, "Hail, King of the Jews!" And they struck Him with their hands.
>
> Pilate then went out again, and said to them, "Behold, I am bringing Him out to you, that you may know that I find no fault in Him."
>
> Then Jesus came out, wearing the crown of thorns and the purple robe. And Pilate said to them, "Behold the Man!"
>
> Therefore, when the chief priests and officers saw Him, they cried out, saying, "Crucify Him, crucify Him!"
>
> Pilate said to them, "You take Him and crucify Him, for I find no fault in Him."
>
> The Jews answered him, "We have a law, and according to our law He ought to die, because He made Himself the Son of God."
>
> Therefore, when Pilate heard that saying, he was the more afraid, and went again into the Praetorium, and said to Jesus, "Where are You from?" But Jesus gave him no answer.
>
> Then Pilate said to Him, "Are You not speaking to me? Do You not know that I have power to crucify You, and power to release You?"
>
> Jesus answered, "You could have no power at all against Me unless it had been given you

from above. Therefore the one who delivered Me to you has the greater sin."

From then on Pilate sought to release Him, but the Jews cried out, saying, "If you let this Man go, you are not Caesar's friend. Whoever makes himself a king speaks against Caesar."

When Pilate therefore heard that saying, he brought Jesus out and sat down in the judgment seat in a place that is called The Pavement, but in Hebrew, Gabbatha. Now it was the Preparation Day of the Passover, and about the sixth hour. And he said to the Jews, "Behold your King!"

But they cried out, "Away with Him, away with Him! Crucify Him!"

Pilate said to them, "Shall I crucify your King?"

The chief priests answered, "We have no king but Caesar!"

Then he delivered Him to them to be crucified. Then they took Jesus and led Him away. (John 19:1–16)

The Human Race Condemns God and Breaks Covenant

Notice the following points in this narrative.

Pilate repeatedly found no fault in Jesus; thus, under Roman law, He was innocent. Yet to pacify the crowd, he mocked Him with a parody of the primary charge against Him, giving Him a robe and crown of thorns. The robe was a farce compared to the robes of God (Ps. 93:1). The crown, twisted from the fruit of the ground cursed because of Adam, pierced the head of its creator (Gen. 3:18). Pilate had the soldiers scourge Him and abuse Him, but the mob still wasn't satisfied.

To Pilate's declaration, "I find no fault in Him," the Jews retorted, "We have a law." It wasn't God's law. It was their own law of self-preservation; they hid behind a religious facade. The Roman Empire found no fault, but inflicted judgment based on Pilate's need for self-preservation. God's kingdom found no fault. But the Jews, also motivated by their own self-preservation, used twisted and distorted laws of their own making to murder the innocent man Jesus, the Son of God.

Finally, in full insurrection against God, they declared their choice: "We have no king but Caesar!"

Matthew's gospel adds even more detail as Matthew describes how the mob, in its bloodlust to condemn Jesus, even invoked condemnation on themselves:

> They all said to him, "Let Him be crucified!"
>
> Then the governor said, "Why, what evil has He done?"
>
> But they cried out all the more, saying, "Let Him be crucified!"
>
> When Pilate saw that he could not prevail at all, but rather that a tumult was rising, he took water and washed his hands before the multitude, saying, "I am innocent of the blood of this just Person. You see to it."
>
> And all the people answered and said, "His blood be on us and on our children."
>
> Then he released Barabbas to them; and

when he had scourged Jesus, he delivered Him
to be crucified. (Matt. 27:22–26)

Thus the Jews, whose fathers had stood before Mount
Sinai and said, "All that the LORD has spoken we will do"
(Ex. 19:3–8), here loudly declared their rejection of His
rule. They would "do" for God no longer. They would have
no king other than the one they chose themselves: "We
have no king but Caesar!" (John 19:15). The crowd fren-
ziedly embraced Rome's proffer of Barabbas, a thief, destroyer, and murderer, and rejected Jesus, God's ordained
king and Savior for the world (John 4:42; 18:36–37).

With their declaration of "His blood be on us and on
our children" (Matt. 27:25) to Pilate—the local ruler of
their chosen kingdom—they annulled the blood covenant
their ancestors had established through offerings at Sinai,
making a new unholy pledge of their own (and their children's) blood, declared to Rome in opposition to God.

I had been taught that it was only the Jews who had
rejected Jesus, as in "He came to His own, and His own
did not receive Him" (John 1:11). But in truth, Jesus had
come to all—to as many as would receive Him and believe
(John 1:12; 3:16–17). Here at Jesus's trial and conviction,
we see all of humanity represented, united in judgment and
condemnation of their creator: Jew and gentile, rich and
poor, noble and common, religious and secular—all were
represented in that assemblage.

But God is greater than all our scheming. He always
seeks out and finds those who are lost, no matter how lost
they are. For all those who will come to God through Jesus,
He once and forever saves completely (Heb. 7:25).

Through His passion and resurrection, Jesus became the surety of a better covenant, initiated by God. The responsibility for perfect obedience in that covenant was now on Jesus. A *surety* is a person who takes responsibility for another's performance of an undertaking. The old covenant was here broken and rejected by men, but was fulfilled through Jesus. As with Abraham, God supplied the offering (Gen. 22:8, 13–14). God has always been for us and never against us. This was the beginning of a new and personal covenant between God and individuals (Luke 22:20). Specifically, it's between God and Jesus on our behalf (1 Tim. 2:3–6). It cannot be broken, and it is better than the old, for He is our surety (Heb. 7:22).

CHAPTER 12

Atonement Is Opened to All

*Therefore, brethren, having boldness to enter the
Holiest by the blood of Jesus, by a new and living
way which He consecrated for us, through the
veil, that is, His flesh, and having a High Priest
over the house of God, let us draw near with a
true heart in full assurance of faith.*
Hebrews 10:19–22

**KEY: Jesus has, in His body, broken down every barrier
and bridged every gulf between God and humankind.**

Jesus was the solution before the problem existed
(Rev. 13:8). Jesus came as the way, the truth, and the
life to a world that had been lost since Adam—believing
lies about God and being dead in their trespasses and sins
(John 14:6). The Trinity (the Father, Son, and Holy Spirit)
was united in their goal to defeat sin, redeem creation, and
conquer death. Jesus, through His blood, overcame our
sin-birthed self-destruction. Sin makes us run away from
God, but God runs toward those victimized by sin. Just
as in the garden, He still calls to Adam (us), "Where are
you?" Jesus didn't save us from God; the Trinity was never
divided. Isaiah states it plainly—Jesus bore *our* wrath.

He was despised and rejected by men,
A Man of sorrows and pain and acquainted
with grief;
And like One from whom men hide their
faces
He was despised, and we did not appreciate
His worth or esteem Him.
But [in fact] He has borne our griefs,
And He has carried our sorrows and pains;
Yet we [ignorantly] assumed that He was
stricken,
Struck down by God and degraded and hu-
miliated [by Him].
But He was wounded for our transgressions,
He was crushed for our wickedness [our sin,
our injustice, our wrongdoing];
The punishment [required] for our well-being
fell on Him,
And by His stripes (wounds) we are healed.
(Isa. 53:3–5 AMP, brackets in the original)

Early in my Christian walk I believed what I had been taught—that Jesus had been sent by God to die to satisfy God's justice—that God struck Him down and, in His justice and because of His holiness, forsook Jesus on the cross. But that is not true. The truth is that He was despised, rejected, and executed by us—mankind (Acts 2:36).

I suspect that for those who know the story, and particularly those who were raised with the same understanding that I had, their well-trained doctrinal alarms are clanging loudly right now, saying, "So what about the cry of Jesus on the cross: 'My God, My God, why have You forsaken Me?' [Matt. 27:46]. It can't get any clearer than that!" To assuage any concerns that I may be wandering off the path of truth, I need to briefly address that difficulty now, although we'll discuss it again later in the book.

Those words of Jesus had also made me uneasy. Deep down and secretly I'd wondered, *If there was a circumstance under which the most perfect and righteous man could be abandoned by God, could I trust that His promise to always be with me [Matt. 28:20] would always be true?* I certainly had the feeling I had been left alone sometimes.

However, this cry of Jesus was spoken in a context of scriptural precedent, cultural practice, and an intimate relationship with His Father. When I saw it that way, instead of as an isolated cry of frustration, it further added to my assurance and sense of security in God's care. In particular, there were four insights that opened my eyes:

1. Jesus wasted no words on the cross; He could barely breathe. He quoted these words from Psalm 22:1—a psalm traditionally recited at Purim, a festival celebrating Israel's deliverance from a foreign power set on their genocide. As the first line was read each year, the people would join the reading, quoting from memory. People knew the psalm that Jesus started. It's a psalm about trusting the Lord when opposition comes and God seems far away. But verse 24 says:

    For He has not despised nor abhorred the
    affliction of the afflicted;
    Nor has He hidden His face from Him;
    But when He cried to Him, He heard.

2. God promises multiple times that He will never leave or forsake those who put their trust in Him (Deut. 31:6, 8; Heb. 13:5–6; 2 Tim. 2:13). If those promises are true for us, wouldn't they also be true for Jesus, who trusted better than any other man?

3. "Hands that shed innocent blood" are an abomination to the Lord (Prov. 6:16–17; Jer. 22:3). God didn't sacrifice Jesus. He didn't violate His own character.

4. "Father, 'into Your hands I commit My spirit'" (Luke 23:46) is another quote from a psalm (Ps. 31:5), which is also enlightening when read in its context. Jesus committed His spirit to His Father, who had not forsaken Him, but was present with Him through His suffering.

Jesus's Submission to His Father

As I looked at Jesus's suffering over this time, I found there was one truth I had to remember in order to continue to see things clearly and avoid serious error—Jesus was inseparable from His Father in His thoughts, words, and actions. His very being was one with the Father (John 17:20–23).

> The worst heresy, next to that of dividing religion and righteousness, is to divide the Father from the Son, in thought or feeling or action or intent; to represent the Son as doing that which the Father does not himself do. If Jesus suffered

for men, it was because his Father suffers for men; only he came close to men through his body and their senses, that he might bring their spirits close to his Father and their Father, so giving them life, and losing what could be lost of his own. He is God our Saviour: it is because God is our Saviour that Jesus is our Saviour.[17]

In Jesus's obedience and submission, as a man, to His Father, God was pleased. Jesus gave Himself as an offering for sin; therefore, the good pleasure of the Lord prospered in Him (Phil. 2:8–9). Jesus had emptied Himself of all glory and all entitlement. He was fully and completely a man, but He was a man fully submitted to and drawing His life from God, His Father. As Jesus said:

> I am the good shepherd. The good shepherd gives His life for the sheep. . . . Therefore My Father loves Me, because I lay down My life that I may take it again. No one takes it from Me, but I lay it down of Myself. I have power to lay it down, and I have power to take it again. This command I have received from My Father. (John 10:11, 17–18)

Jesus laid down His life for us like the good shepherd who gives his life for the sheep. If Jesus's life had been taken involuntarily, it would not have been an offering.

We often refer to Jesus's "work on the cross." What I had missed was that the Father was intimately with Him the whole time, empowering Him to completion. God the

Father was "in Christ reconciling the world to Himself" (2 Cor. 5:19). Jesus's real work on the cross was obedience. Through that obedience God reconciled the world, restored life, and exalted Jesus. In the same way, as we obey, God works in and through us for His glory and our good (Phil. 2:5–13).

Jesus's Prayer for Those Who Will Follow Him

Somewhere between the Last Supper and the garden of Gethsemane, while Jesus was still with His disciples, He prayed. This prayer, recorded in John 17, is often called the High Priestly Prayer because it was His prayer of intercession. Jesus interceded for His disciples, as well as for all those after them who would believe in Him. In the first part, Jesus prayed to His Father about Himself, telling Him that He had finished what God had sent Him to do. He had done it well and had prepared His disciples to carry on. In the second part, He prayed for all who follow Him in faith, for their protection, purity, and power. But above all, He prayed for their unity, not only with each other, but most importantly, with God.

> I do not pray for these alone, but also for those who will believe in Me through their word; that they all may be one, as You, Father, are in Me, and I in You; that they also may be one in Us, that the world may believe that You sent Me. And the glory which You gave Me I have given them, that they may be one just as We are one: I in them, and You in Me; that they may be made perfect in one, and that the world may

know that You have sent Me, and have loved them as You have loved Me. (John 17:20–23)

Jesus prayed that the same inseparable oneness that existed between Jesus and His Father would also be true for all of us who believe in Jesus so that others can believe also and know the same love.

Jesus Submits in Prayer

In Gethsemane, Jesus separated Himself from the disciples and prayed what is probably His most famous prayer, aside from the Lord's Prayer. Jesus trusted His Father intimately and poured out His soul to Him.

> He said to His disciples, "Sit here while I pray." And He took Peter, James, and John with Him, and He began to be troubled and deeply distressed. Then He said to them, "My soul is exceedingly sorrowful, even to death. Stay here and watch."
>
> He went a little farther, and fell on the ground, and prayed that if it were possible, the hour might pass from Him. And He said, "Abba, Father, all things are possible for You. Take this cup away from Me; nevertheless, not what I will, but what You will."
>
> Then He came and found them sleeping, and said to Peter, "Simon, are you sleeping? Could you not watch one hour? Watch and pray, lest you enter into temptation. The spirit indeed is willing, but the flesh is weak."

> Again He went away and prayed, and
> spoke the same words. And when He returned,
> He found them asleep again, for their eyes were
> heavy; and they did not know what to answer
> Him.
>
> Then He came the third time and said to
> them, "Are you still sleeping and resting? It is
> enough! The hour has come; behold, the Son
> of Man is being betrayed into the hands of sin-
> ners." (Mark 14:32–41)

Mark says He prayed that the hour might pass from
Him. It was not *death* that He dreaded. His life couldn't be
taken from Him. He alone had the power to lay it down
(John 10:18). He dreaded the *hour* of the cross—that moment when sin was going to be put on Him—when He
would be made sin for us (2 Cor. 5:21.) Mark makes the
"hour" and the "cup" synonymous. The cup contained the
sins of the whole world. More than death itself and the
horrible suffering of crucifixion, this is what we have trouble comprehending: Jesus, holy and pure, was made *sin* for
us. There on the cross, the sin of humanity was put on
Him: not in some abstract legal manner, but in *reality*. We
can't imagine the horror He felt when that sin was placed
upon Him.

He was not asking to escape the cross; He was asking
for God's will to be done. Matthew records the second
time He prayed: "O My Father, if this cup cannot pass
away from Me unless I drink it, Your will be done" (Matt.
26:42). He was accepting it.

Jesus was completely human, and in His humanity, He

felt a repugnance; He felt the awful horror of having the sin of the world placed on Him, and He recoiled from it. But He committed Himself to the Father. He had come to do the Father's will.

Jesus's Crucifixion

Throughout the physical agony of the cross and the crushing spiritual agony of the sin He carried, Jesus continued to shine forth the character of His Father.

When Jesus took on the sin of the world (2 Cor. 5:21), He saw as Adam saw after he fell, with his spiritual vision distorted by sin. Although His perception of His Father's presence was obscured, His Father never abandoned Him (Ps. 37:25; 2 Cor. 5:19; John 10:30; 16:32; Ps. 22–24). Jesus overcame His deceitful human emotions and persevered by His faith in the Father He knew well. Unlike the first Adam, He ran *toward* His Father and not away—and committed His spirit to His Father's care.

The Way to God Is Opened

Jesus's death removed the physical barriers of the Mosaic covenant. The way to God was now through Jesus, the door, symbolized by the tearing of the heavy veil between the Holy Place and the Holy of Holies in the temple. Starting with God in response to His Son's offering in faith, it was torn from the top down. Dead souls came to life, and eyes of understanding started to open, even among the gentiles.

Then, behold, the veil of the temple was torn in

two from top to bottom; and the earth quaked, and the rocks were split, and the graves were opened; and many bodies of the saints who had fallen asleep were raised; and coming out of the graves after His resurrection, they went into the holy city and appeared to many.

So when the centurion and those with him, who were guarding Jesus, saw the earthquake and the things that had happened, they feared greatly, saying, "Truly this was the Son of God!" (Matt. 27:51–54)

Joseph of Arimathea, a secret disciple of Jesus, had asked special permission to take possession of the body of Jesus. He and Nicodemus prepared the body for burial according to Jewish custom. With spices and linen wrapping, they honored the body and laid it in a new sepulcher nearby (John 19:38–42).

I mentioned that at the moment of Jesus's death, the veil of the temple was torn in two; therefore, the way that had been closed opened. Where did that way lead? It opened into the Holy of Holies, where the ark of the covenant had originally been housed. (The ark had been removed sometime between the first and second temples.)

To understand why this is important, we need some background. For the Jews, the ark of the covenant of the Lord was the most sacred object imaginable. It was an ornate, gold-covered box built to specifications given by God to Moses (Ex. 25:10). Jewish tradition states that stored within the ark were the broken tablets inscribed with the Ten Commandments written by God, along with the second set of tablets dictated by God and inscribed by Moses (Talmud Bava Batra 14b). A pot of manna and Aaron's rod were also in the ark (Heb. 9:4).

The ark was covered by the golden *kapporet*, the lid, which was adorned with two golden cherubim facing each other and looking down on the central part of the lid, which was called the mercy seat.

The ark and its *kapporet* were the only objects in the Holy of Holies. The high priest entered this inner sanctum only one day a year, on the Day of Atonement. On that day he would wear special garments made of linen, and he would spread the blood of a young bull and a goat on the mercy seat to make atonement for the sins of all of Israel (Lev. 16:4, 14–16).

The ark was the focal point of God's relationship with His people, and it was from there that God would speak. God told Moses, "There I will meet with you, and I will speak with you from above the mercy seat, from between the two cherubim which are on the ark of the Testimony, about everything which I will give you in commandment to the children of Israel" (Ex. 25:22).

Take a moment to remember with me the last time we saw cherubim. It was when Adam and Eve had been exiled from the garden. God "placed cherubim at the east of the garden of Eden, and a flaming sword which turned every way, to guard the way to the tree of life" (Gen. 3:24). The tree of life is always associated with the presence of God. Here at the mercy seat, the way to God has also been guarded.

Mary Sees Her Salvation

So after that brief digression into temple furnishings and liturgy, let's return to the tomb of Jesus. The women came early on the first day of the week, expecting to find a body. Instead they saw the great stone rolled away from the mouth of the tomb. That stone was rolled away to let the women and the disciples in, not to let Jesus out! Mary Magdalene was the first to see Jesus resurrected.

> But Mary stood outside by the tomb weeping, and as she wept she stooped down and looked into the tomb. And she saw two angels in white sitting, one at the head and the other at the feet, where the body of Jesus had lain. Then they said to her, "Woman, why are you weeping?"
>
> She said to them, "Because they have taken away my Lord, and I do not know where they have laid Him."
>
> Now when she had said this, she turned around and saw Jesus standing there. (John 20:11–14)

There in the garden tomb, Mary saw in reality what existed only in symbol on the lid of the ark in the Holy of Holies. She saw the place of atonement. She saw the slab holding the blood-stained linen graveclothes, with the napkin that had covered His head folded together and to the side (John 20:5–7). Two angels were sitting there: one at the head and one at the foot. Jesus was gone; only the linen graveclothes remained. The vestments of the high priest of Israel were made of linen (Lev. 16:4).

Mary had seen the mercy seat of God. The offering of atonement was finished. God no longer had to meet with men only between the cherubim. Now He could meet as a friend. When Mary turned, she saw Jesus.

That Hebrew word for mercy seat, *kapporet,* when translated into Greek (in Rom. 3:25 and Heb. 9:5), is our old friend *hilasterion*: propitiation. The mercy seat was the place of propitiation and meeting. In a sense, God was propitiated at Jesus's death, and humankind at His resurrection (Rom. 4:24–25).

The book of Hebrews tells us that the tabernacle, and later the temple, were only symbols of a greater tabernacle existing in heaven (Heb. 9:8–12, 24). Jesus applied His own blood to the heavenly mercy seat in the heavenly tabernacle as our eternal atonement and redemption (Heb. 9). We, therefore, by faith in the blood of Jesus, can come boldly into intimacy with God with a clear conscience. In Jesus we have a better covenant than the old.

> "This is the covenant that I will make with them after those days, says the LORD: I will put My laws into their hearts, and in their minds I will write them," then He adds, "Their sins and their lawless deeds I will remember no more." Now where there is remission of these, there is no longer an offering for sin.
>
> Therefore, brethren, having boldness to enter the Holiest by the blood of Jesus, by a new and living way which He consecrated for us, through the veil, that is, His flesh, and having a High Priest over the house of God, let us draw near with a true heart in full assurance of

faith, having our hearts sprinkled from an evil
conscience and our bodies washed with pure
water. Let us hold fast the confession of our
hope without wavering, for He who promised
is faithful. (Heb. 10:16–23)

Jesus was fully man and fully God. As a man, He submitted to death and offered Himself to God. As God, He
submitted Himself to the judgment and sentencing of humankind. "Greater love has no one than this, than to lay
down one's life for his friends" (John 15:13). "But God
demonstrates His own love toward us, in that while we
were still sinners, Christ died for us" (Rom. 5:8). Jesus had
greater love than a man because He died for those who were
not His friends. The peace, the propitiation, brought by
the Prince of Peace (Isa. 9:6; John 14:27) went in both
directions, bringing peace with God and peace with men.

Christians commemorate these events through the sacrament of Holy Communion (the Eucharist). The bread
represents Jesus's torn body on the cross and, when broken, corresponds to the torn veil, opening the way to the
Holy of Holies and the presence of God. The cup stands
for Jesus's blood and corresponds to the accepted offering
of His life. That offering was His life; the blood itself is
only the representation of something greater. God doesn't
want offerings of blood; He wants lives in offering (1 Sam.
15:22–24; Jer. 7:21–23). It is because of Jesus's propitiation offered in obedience that we, in Him, can walk boldly
through that veil to the mercy seat of heaven without fear
and without shame.

CHAPTER 13

The Beautiful Way

Run, John, and work, the law commands,
Yet finds me neither feet nor hands;
But sweeter news the gospel brings,
It bids me fly, and lends me wings.[18]
—John Berridge

KEY: It is through our own obedience unto death that we become free.

Hebrews tells us, "Without faith it is impossible to please Him, for he who comes to God must believe that He is, and that He is a rewarder of those who diligently seek Him" (Heb. 11:6). We cannot come to God with any assurance unless we first believe God exists, that when we get there we will be rewarded, and that all the difficulties encountered on the way will have been worth it.

This is the same pattern we saw Jesus follow on the cross. Even during the dark time when He no longer sensed His Father's presence, He continued to focus on God and press forward in faith. He trusted in the character of the Father He already knew well—the One He knew would never leave Him or abandon Him no matter the circumstances. We have that same assurance. Jesus also knew He would be rewarded. His suffering, far from being meaningless, would bring light and life to the whole world. It was for the joy set before Him that He endured the cross and disdained its shame (Heb. 12:2). What was that joy? Through it all He brought "many sons to glory" (Heb. 2:10).

Learning Obedience

There is a statement in Hebrews 5:8–9 that may seem strange at first: "Though He was a Son, yet He learned obedience by the things which He suffered. And having been perfected, He became the author of eternal salvation to all who obey Him." What does that mean? Jesus's whole life had been a model of perfect obedience to His Father. How could He learn obedience any more perfectly? Also, since Christ was free from sin, wouldn't obedience come naturally to Him already? Let's expand it by looking at the whole passage in the Amplified version:

> For every high priest chosen from among men is appointed [to act] on behalf of men in things relating to God, so that he may offer both gifts and sacrifices for sins. He is able to deal gently with the spiritually ignorant and misguided, since he is also subject to human weakness; and because of this [human weakness] he is required to offer sacrifices for sins, for himself as well as for the people. And besides, one does not appropriate for himself the honor [of being high priest], but he who is called by God, just as Aaron was. . . .
>
> In the days of His earthly life, Jesus offered up both [specific] petitions and [urgent]

supplications [for that which He needed] with
fervent crying and tears to the one who was
[always] able to save Him from death, and
He was heard because of His reverent submission toward God [His sinlessness and His un-
failing determination to do the Father's will].
Although He was a Son [who had never been
disobedient to the Father], He learned [active,
special] obedience through what He suffered.
And having been made perfect [uniquely
equipped and prepared as Savior and retaining
His integrity amid opposition], He became the
source of eternal salvation [an eternal inheri-
tance] to all those who obey Him, being desig-
nated by God as High Priest according to the
order of Melchizedek. (Heb. 5:1–4, 7–10 AMP,
brackets in the original)

A high priest was chosen from among men and called
by God to act on behalf of the people in all things relating
to God. To act effectively and compassionately on behalf of
others, he must be able to, out of his personal experience,
deal gently with the spiritually ignorant and misguided—
the lost.

When the Bible speaks of Christ learning obedience, it
is talking about His *experiencing* obedience. Notice it says
He learned *obedience*, not that He learned *to obey*. John
Owen, a Puritan theologian of the seventeenth century, explains:

The Lord Christ learned obedience when he
experienced it in practice. One special kind of

> obedience is intended here, namely a submis-
> sion to great, hard, and terrible things, accom-
> panied by patience and quiet endurance, and
> faith for deliverance from them. This, Christ
> could not have experience of, except by suffer-
> ing the things he had to pass through, exercis-
> ing [employing] God's grace in them all.[19]

We can learn to obey as a mere outward action out of duty. But when we learn obedience, that has to do with the heart. The attitude becomes the action. An example is in marriage: submission is more than an action; it's a heart orientation. You can't just "submit." You have to submit to each other with your heart, actions, and head, depending on God's grace as you go through difficulties, trials, and dilemmas together along the way.

I used to think that Jesus, even though He was a man, had certain advantages that I didn't have, especially in obedience and resisting temptation. Although I read that Jesus was "in all points tempted as we are, yet without sin" (Heb. 4:15), it seemed to me, on some of my more discouraged days, that He had missed out on some unique problems because He didn't have a spouse and children and didn't have to deal with modern technology. It was true that Jesus's close friend (Lazarus) died, but in my cynicism and hurt, it seemed His grief couldn't have been too bad since He knew He would raise Him from the dead (John 11:11).

Of course, my feelings were inaccurate. Jesus had all the frustrations of training His disciples. He only had a limited amount of time with them, and they weren't the quickest learners. They kept missing what He was trying to teach them. He also knew grief. Most likely He had lived through the death of His father, Joseph, and experienced that loss with the rest of His family. But to me, Jesus's biggest advantage was that He had His Father guiding His every step, never leaving Him and always showing Him what to do. That was something I knew I wasn't experiencing. There were many times I seemed completely deaf to God's voice, and I felt alone.

On the cross, Jesus experienced what each of us has felt: disconnection from God—a feeling that He's off somewhere, uncaring, and we are left alone. It can be a subtle uneasiness that maybe we did something unpleasing and lost favor. Everyone has felt that, but we can take comfort that Jesus knows the feeling. We can also take comfort that the same obedience and trust in God's promises that Jesus had will also carry us through those lying feelings. God has promised to never leave us or forsake us. Jesus was human like us and asks us to do the same as He did, and to do it in the same way: in obedience and in faith in our loving Father.

We follow in Jesus's steps. His obedience as a man, empowered by the grace of God, qualified Him to act on behalf of men in things relating to God so that He could offer both gifts and sacrifices for sins. The first and only sacrifice He offered was Himself to God. The gift He offered was also Himself—to us. He became the source of eternal salvation (an eternal inheritance) to all those who obey Him.

To all who obey Him. What is it about obedience? It seems to have been essential for Jesus to "learn it" as part of what was needed to defeat sin in His flesh on our behalf, and now the author of Hebrews declares it is also essential to our attaining salvation. This is the same principle James refers to in the first part of his epistle:

> My brethren, count it all joy when you fall into various trials, knowing that the testing of your faith produces patience. But let patience have its perfect work, that you may be perfect and complete, lacking nothing. . . .
>
> Blessed is the man who endures temptation; for when he has been approved, he will receive the crown of life which the Lord has promised to those who love Him. (James 1:2–4, 12)

Approved here is the same Greek word used in 2 Timothy 2:15: "Be diligent to present yourself approved to God, a worker who does not need to be ashamed, rightly dividing the word of truth." The word means "approved after trial" or "assayed." To assay is to analyze a metal or ore to determine its ingredients or quality.

So, then, is obedience a way to gain salvation by our works? Absolutely not. But a salvation that's working produces a measurable difference in our behavior. To be saved implies we were saved from something or some place. We are saved by grace, through faith; it is a gift of God and not from our works. By that grace, and in Christ through faith, we are new creatures (2 Cor. 5:17).

Moving to a New Kingdom

To appropriate what God has provided in His grace, there must be a radical changing of kingdoms. When we shift our faith from ourselves to God, we relinquish control. We step off the throne of the kingdom of self, where we were sure we knew what was right and wrong and good and evil and where we had the illusion of control. We abdicate. We repent and say to God, "Only You know truly what is good and evil, because You are *good*. I submit my will and my kingdom to Yours, and I will obey You, acknowledging that, as You are good, Your plans are good, whether I can see it or not right now. I will trust You and obey You. I declare You to be my Lord, replacing myself."

Real obedience is from the heart. It's not just words nor only actions. To obey sin is death. To obey God is life (Rom. 6:16). Sin itself was not a problem for God; He is not tempted (James 1:13). But it's a killer problem for us. We have no hope of the death of sin in us without the death of Christ. The question is, How does His death become effectual for us, killing sin in our mortal bodies?

In Galatians 2:20, Paul says, "I have been crucified with Christ; it is no longer I who live, but Christ lives in me; and the life which I now live in the flesh I live by faith in the Son of God, who loved me and gave Himself for me." How am I crucified with Christ? By faith. Paul also said, "Do you not know that to whom you present yourselves slaves to obey, you are that one's slaves whom you obey, whether of sin leading to death, or of obedience leading to righteousness?" (Rom. 6:16). We have a choice of whom to serve: sin and self-rule leading to death, or God, with an obedience leading to righteousness and life.

Jesus emptied Himself and became "of no reputation": a servant. As a man, He humbled Himself and became obedient to death, a public death on the cross. It was not through His death, but through His obedience that culminated in death, that sin was defeated in the flesh of men (Rom. 5:19). In His obedience, through the voluntary sacrifice of His life, represented by His blood, we have been redeemed.

Working Out Our Salvation

Our redemption has been purchased, but our full salvation is more of an ongoing untangling of habits, thought patterns (Rom. 12:2–3), and beliefs, learning to trust, obey, and know God more and more (Rom. 8:29–31). Salvation is a journey of growing trust and obedience.

> Therefore, my beloved, as you have always obeyed, not as in my presence only, but now much more in my absence, work out your own salvation with fear and trembling; for it is God who works in you both to will and to do for His good pleasure. Do all things without complaining and disputing, that you may become blameless and harmless, children of God without fault in the midst of a crooked and perverse generation, among whom you shine as lights in the world, holding fast the word of life. (Phil. 2:12–16)

Salvation is like finding that you're lost deep in a cave with no light. You're disoriented, blind, and hopeless. Suddenly a voice speaks. It is Jesus, who says, "Follow Me. I've been here before. I know the way out." You're somewhat skeptical, but there is no other hope, so you follow. He directs you inch by inch through the blackness. You think you see a light, but He turns you away from it. You have doubts, but you follow. It was only phosphorescence glowing on the walls. Gradually you see real light dimly and start to gain confidence that you can find your way on your own, but He leads you around pitfalls you still don't see. He comes after you when you start to stray. Gradually you transfer more and more of your trust to Him until you're fully free. Then you see you are not alone because He has already "brought many sons to glory" (Heb. 2:10).

You see, when we struggle against sin—which produces death—we are actually struggling *to* the Father, who is life. But beyond our own uncomfortable choice to deny ourselves, there is really no struggle since Jesus is the way. We go *in* Him—the one who has been there, who came and found us, and who returns with us.

Jesus and the Holy Spirit lead, and we are to follow. It takes focus, attentiveness, and obedience. We are easily distracted and then become vulnerable to attack and discouragement. We are saved by grace (there *is* a way out), but it requires faith. We must follow in trust. Grace is a gift available to all, but faith is work and attention to detail. The evidence of faith is works, specifically doing the works that God has prepared for us to do (Eph. 2:10). The essence of faith is obedience: you do what the person you say you have faith in tells you to do. Who you obey reveals who holds your faith. Peter describes the change: "For you were like sheep going astray, but have now returned to the Shepherd and Overseer of your souls" (1 Peter 2:25).

We must follow in His steps. Each time we are tempted, we have a choice. Will we be led astray by our own lusts

(James 1:13–15) or will we follow the "Shepherd and Overseer of [our] souls"? Each time we deny ourselves by denying our unrighteous desires and taking up our cross (Mark 8:34), we follow Jesus in His path to the cross. We, like Him, are called to be obedient to the point of death. When we, in obedience to God, willingly submit our bodies, our passions, our desires, and our sins to death, we are in Him in His obedience on the cross. This is how we are crucified together with Him (Gal. 2:20; 5:24; Rom. 6:3–14; 8:5–14).

Justice Is Satisfied Only through Our Death in Christ

Putting to death our old self is intensely personal. It is not an abstract operation done at a distance. Jesus did not die for us in the sense that He was our substitute while we waited patiently in the waiting room to hear that the deed was done, justice was satisfied, and we were free. No! We die with Him and in Him. That is the only way justice could be done, righteousness satisfied, and mercy bestowed.

Christ absolutely died for our benefit, but it is foolishness to believe He died *instead* of us. If we didn't die with Him, we could never be raised with Him into newness of life. Secondly, our conscience could never be cleansed because our heart knows our guilt and its penalty. Having another pay by proxy does not satisfy our heart's personal need for justice. Our old accusing conscience must die with our old nature, *with* Christ, for us to be free of its condemnation.

I still hear preachers and teachers tell people, just as I had been told, to stop feeling condemned. They tell people to get free of their feelings of guilt and shame by accepting the facts and believing they're forgiven. The implication is that if people are still feeling vague guilt and uneasiness about their salvation, that means they're not believing that "Jesus did it all." These teachers err in thinking that believing is attaining undoubting mental acknowledgment of a fact instead of what the Bible means when it says believe: an entrustment of our all, including our very life, to God.

Let me be blunt. Christianity is not about rationalizing ourselves out of feelings of guilt and condemnation. Mental agreement that Jesus "paid the price" does not and cannot do it. My guilt disappears only when *I* pay the price, when justice has been righteously accomplished in me. If the wages of my sin is death, then death is satisfied and releases me from condemnation only when I die. Can I do this myself? Can I take any credit for my own salvation? No! Because the person that must die is *me*. But if I'm dead, how can I live? It is only by being *in* Christ, both in His death and in His resurrection, so that now the life I live *from* and *in* is His life; mine is gone (Gal. 2:20). "There is therefore now no condemnation to those who are in Christ Jesus, who do not walk according to the flesh, but according to the Spirit" (Rom. 8:1). The walk and work of our new life is ongoing. We, through Christ's death, are freed from sin. However, some days it seems like our old ways still cling to us like a dead octopus. The extrication process is work (Rom. 6:4–14).

Jesus had to come as a man, in the flesh, to deal with sin. Sin is the scourge of men, not of God, and can be dealt with only in the flesh. Killing sin and self-will is the work of the living. As one old preacher said, "Be killing sin or it will be killing you!"[20] Where men are dead—as all unbelievers, the best of them, are dead—sin is *alive* and will live (Rom. 5:21; 6:12). Thus, be encouraged to know that if you're fighting sin, you're alive! But if sin reigns unopposed, you are dead no matter how lively your sin makes you feel.

Resisting sin is active, not passive. Hebrews 2:1–4 exhorts us not to neglect our salvation journey. It must be attended to. Easy believing is not in the Bible and does not produce new creations (2 Cor. 5:17). A man must be in Christ, the man, for re-creation (Eph. 2:10). If we aren't united in His death, we cannot be united in His resurrection (Rom. 6:1–14). We must be united in His resurrection because if we are not raised with Him, we have no life. "If Christ is not risen, your faith is futile; you are still in your sins!" (1 Cor. 15:17).

Modern Christendom tends to oversimplify this concept and insists that saying a "sinner's prayer" is enough. As long as that one vital step is done, ongoing discipline and discipleship seem to be treated as optional. However, simply acknowledging our sin is not sufficient to transform us, and it is definitely not enough to motivate us to be faithful disciples. For example, Romans 10:9–10 is often quoted as the blueprint to get saved: "If you confess with your mouth the Lord Jesus and believe in your heart that God has raised Him from the dead, you will be saved. For with the heart one believes unto righteousness, and with the mouth confession is made unto salvation."

What's missing in that formula is the context. Verse 9 is the second half of a sentence Paul wrote in which, for the first half (vv. 6–8), he had been quoting from Deuteronomy 30, where God promises the Israelites prosperity if they keep His commandments. There God, through Moses, outlined a covenant and set options before the people: life and good or death and evil. Obedience to God's law within that covenant wasn't to be coercive, but was to be internal, intimate, and life-giving.

Keeping those commandments was a commitment not just to being part of Israel, but to being separate from other nations, being committed to a different way of living, and taking a stand to eradicate unrighteousness in their lives (Deut. 20:1–3). In the same way, a commitment to Christ requires a renunciation of our old ways and a sober-minded submission to God.

Our Invitation into the Life of Christ

Those same choices are set before us: life and good or death and evil. There is no neutrality in this contest because each one of us is the prize. There are only two choices, only two kingdoms to which we can pledge our allegiance: the kingdom of self—which is, by default, the kingdom of Satan—or the kingdom of God. Because of our father, Adam, we all start our lives in the kingdom of self.

As we renounce our own throne and kingdom, abdicate, and make Jesus our Lord—the sole king and arbiter of our lives, we are promised that His commandments for living (His Word) will be always available to us—in our mouths and in our hearts, that we may be able to do it (Deut. 30:14).

We are invited into Christ's life through God's grace,

and it is accomplished through our deliberate submission and obedience to Him through faith. We accept His invitation, through faith and through obedience, to His purposes. We "share in His sufferings." Throughout His passion, Jesus demonstrated that His sufferings were beyond physical as He took on the sin of the world and died to it.

We also are to present our sinful selves to death, but only in Christ (Rom. 8:13; Gal. 2:20; 6:14–15). Presenting ourselves to death outside of Christ, even when disguised as a justifiably self-imposed penance or fasting, is an exercise in self-righteous futility. Self has no problem with a self-supervised execution it can be proud of. In the end, that kind of suffering is for nothing (1 Cor. 13:3). However, when we die with Christ, then we are also raised with Him. Once we are in Him, we go where He goes.

Being in Christ is inseparable from obedience. Thus, one of the first things asked of a new believer is a public act of obedience: the sacrament of baptism. In baptism, the believer goes down into the water declaring his death to his old life (publicly renouncing his own rule), and he rises out of the water as a declaration of his new birth into a new kingdom and under a new father-king (Rom. 6:3–7). In Christ is our newness of life and our re-creation to victory over sin. However, just as with Cain, sin still crouches at the door with its desire for us. Our new life in Christ is to be characterized by watchful, joyful dependence. We have been set free from slavery to sin, but are still susceptible to temptation in all areas where we allow it to have a voice.

> Now if we died with Christ, we believe that we
> shall also live with Him, knowing that Christ,

having been raised from the dead, dies no more. Death no longer has dominion over Him. For the death that He died, He died to sin once for all; but the life that He lives, He lives to God. Likewise you also, reckon yourselves to be dead indeed to sin, but alive to God in Christ Jesus our Lord.

Therefore do not let sin reign in your mortal body, that you should obey it in its lusts. And do not present your members as instruments of unrighteousness to sin, but present yourselves to God as being alive from the dead, and your members as instruments of righteousness to God. For sin shall not have dominion over you, for you are not under law but under grace. (Rom. 6:8–14)

That heavy veil in the temple wasn't torn from top to bottom and that heavy stone wasn't rolled away in that garden tomb to let God out; the way was opened to let us in. The women and the disciples could walk into the tomb, where until then, death had always reigned without challenge. Now when they walked in, there was no death there. There were only angels with good news to men, making full circle their announcement in the shepherds' field of Bethlehem at Jesus's birth: The Savior is risen. Peace.

Also there in the empty tomb was the figure of the mercy seat, now open to all. Jesus, Immanuel, is with us forever (Matt. 1:23; 28:20; Eph. 3:16–19).

CHAPTER 14

A New World of Freedom:
Suddenly Opened

Free at last, Free at last,
Thank God Almighty
I'm Free at last.[21]
—Martin Luther King Jr.

KEY: The paradoxical culture of becoming a free slave of righteousness.

The gospel is the good news to us of a new king and a new kingdom. When we understand that, everything changes. For us who believe, the old kingdom is gone, replaced by the new. We have been freed from our pasts, have been re-created, and have become new citizens of God's kingdom (2 Cor. 5:17). This was the message Jesus sent His disciples out to preach: the gospel of the kingdom.

Jesus borrowed a Latin word that the Romans of His day used to describe "one who is sent out of": *apostolus* (Luke 6:13). The Romans of Jesus's day ruled most of the known world. As Rome expanded its territory, the leaders of the empire realized that unless these newly conquered people were assimilated into Roman ways, they would eventually revert back to their previous culture and rebel. *Apostoli* were sent out to engraft the culture of Rome into the new territory. In the same way, Jesus appointed apostles to announce His kingdom and demonstrate its culture—teaching the new citizens to follow everything Jesus had commanded them (Matt. 28:19–20). God Himself effects the transfer. "He has delivered us from the power of darkness and conveyed us into the kingdom of the Son of His love" (Col. 1:13).

You Were Bought at a Price

How did we become free? This is a question that had nagged at me for years. I had always been taught that Jesus had "paid the price" and somehow had given His life as a "ransom for all" (1 Tim. 2:6; Matt. 20:28; 1 Cor. 6:20). But who or what was demanding the ransom? To whom was it paid? By now it had become clear to me that it couldn't be God. He wasn't the one holding us captive, and He certainly wouldn't have sent His only Son in payment of a ransom to Himself! Yet our ransom has been paid, our prison door has been opened, and we are no longer slaves to sin (Rom. 6:20). Christ has triumphed, and we are risen with Him into new life (1 Cor. 15:55–57). But how?

Our slave price was paid to *death*, which had laid claim to us through sin. The gatekeeper of death is the devil, who, along with our own leftover carnal impulses, entices us to yield to sin and earn its wages. He is our tempter, accuser, and adversary. He feeds and encourages our sin-twisted perceptions and desires (James 1:13–15).

However, for a long time I had believed that the devil was probably the one being paid off. I based that on my mistaken assumption[22] that the serpent in the garden was the devil himself. Under that presupposition, when Adam and Eve gave in to the serpent's temptation, they shifted their obedience to the devil, thus putting all humans under the lordship of Satan. In turn, Satan demanded the death of a perfect sacrifice in return for our freedom. However, now I can see at least four problems with that view:

1. It's clear that Jesus came to destroy the devil and his works. Jesus did not come to pay blackmail to the devil (Heb. 2:14–15; 1 John 3:8).

2. If Satan had dominion over the earth and all creation, why would he give that up, no matter how perfect the sacrifice? After all, he wanted to be like God, to be lord. Why would Satan find any type of sacrifice that resulted in the redemption of mankind acceptable or desirable?

3. Why would God negotiate? Psalm 24:1 says, "The earth is the Lord's, and all its fullness, the world and those who dwell therein." Adam never had any ownership to give away. He was put in the garden as a steward (Gen. 2:15). As a steward, any dominion or authority he possessed came from the owner as a trust, not as a gift. God was under no obligation to relinquish ownership because of Adam's sin. As a free agent, Adam had bound his life and the lives of his descendants to death, not to the serpent, through his sin.

4. The fear of death kept humanity subject to bondage (Heb. 2:15). Therefore, if death wasn't satisfied, we could never be free.

The truth was that the the serpent was merely the instrument that presented the temptation that led to the real extortioner-executioner: death. Death held our debt, and through it, kept us in slavery (Gal. 5:1).

Jesus made full atonement for us on the cross, and through Him we are justified before God. However, for many of us, those concepts remain abstract. We know conversion and justification occur because we know our hearts change. A new love for God and compassion for our fellow man appear almost spontaneously. Our senses are opened to see God's truths and evidence of God's presence. Our consciences are cleared from sin, guilt, and shame. But as we go on, we soon find that what the Bible calls salvation is a process.

Freedom Can Be Uncomfortable

The new life we receive is real, but we don't know how to walk in it. Just as newly released slaves don't know how to live as free men, so newly saved men don't know how to walk in their new reality (Rom. 6:4). For example, in 1865 when the slaves were freed at the end of the American Civil War, they had trouble even comprehending their new world of freedom, much less being able to function in it.

> The day of freedom come around just [like] any other day, except the Master say for me to bring up the horses, we is going to town. That's when he hears about the slaves being free. We gets to the town and the Master goes into the store. It's pretty early but the streets was filled with folks

talking and I wonder what makes the Master in such a hurry when he comes out of the store. He gets on his horse and tells me to follow fast. When we gets back to the plantation he sounds the horn calling the slaves. They come in from the fields and meet 'round back of the kitchen building that stood separate from the Master's house. They all keeps quiet while the Master talks! "You-all is free now, and all the rest of the slaves is free too. Nobody owns you now and nobody going to wup you anymore!" That was good news, I reckon, but nobody know what to do about it. The crops was mostly in and the Master wants the folks to stay 'til the crop is finished. They talk about it the rest of that day. They wasn't no celebration 'round the place, but they wasn't no work after the Master tells us we is free. Nobody leave the place though. Not 'til in the fall when the work is through. Then some of us go into the town and gets work 'cause everybody knows the Allison slaves was the right kind of folks to have around. That was the first money I earn and then I have to learn how to spend it. That was the hardest part 'cause the prices was high and the wages was low. (William Hutson, enslaved in Georgia, interviewed in Oklahoma, 1937)[23]

Some of the freed slaves stayed on their plantations because they couldn't imagine doing otherwise. There are records of some who, even after they had been freed and knew they were free, still went to the master's house to ask for a pass to leave the plantation. Others wandered, trying their new freedom a little bit at a time. The door to freedom was open before them and all the legalities had been taken care of, but to survive as free men they had to learn a new culture, they had to leave old habits, and they had to renew their minds to a new existence.

> I remember so well how the roads was full of folks walking and walking along when the n——s were freed. Didn't know where they was going. Just going to see about something else somewhere else. Meet a body in the road and they ask, "Where you going?" "Don't know." "What you going to do?" "Don't know." And then sometimes we would meet a white man and he would say, "How you like to come work on my farm?" And we say, "I don't know." And then maybe he say, "If you come work for me on my farm, when the crops is in I give you five bushels of corn, five gallons of molasses, some ham-meat, and all your clothes and vittals while you works for me." Alright! That's what I do. And then something begins to work up here (touching his forehead with his fingers). I begins to think and to know things. And I know then I could make a living for my own self, and I never had to be a slave no more. (Robert Falls, enslaved in North Carolina, interviewed in Tennessee, ca. 1937)[24]

In one day, the slaves were freed. As one of them was quoted, "We was free. Just like that, we was free!" It is the same for those who believe. Old things pass away, and all things become new (2 Cor. 5:17). This transformation is by faith, and the new birth (as Jesus described it to Nicodemus) is instantaneous. That person immediately becomes alive spiritually and becomes part of God's family.

Although many people refer to that initial event as "getting saved," the Bible more often describes salvation as a longer process. For example, to as many as received Jesus and believed, He gave the right to become children of God (John 1:12). Paul told the Philippians to "work out your own salvation with fear and trembling" (Phil. 2:12).

The kingdom of God is a spiritual kingdom (John 18:36), so as children in a new realm of being, with a new culture and a new family, there is much to learn! This is why the Great Commission of Matthew 28:19–20 emphasizes teaching and training over soul collecting. Believers grow through discipleship and mentoring.

Saved from What?

Before we go further, it's important to know what we're being saved *from*. Jesus completed our atonement for sin and became our propitiation to God on the cross, but the Bible also talks about our salvation as an ongoing operation. God is not the one from whom we are being saved. God is well pleased with the finished work of His Son.

Paul says, "So then, with the mind I myself serve the law of God, but with the flesh the law of sin" (Rom. 7:25). There are two opposing laws at work: the law of God and the law of sin. James refers to the law of God as the "law of liberty" (James 1:25; 2:12). The "law of sin," in Romans 8:2, is also called "the law of sin and death."

Some people have proposed that the "law of sin and death" is the Mosaic law. It is true that the law defines sin (Rom. 7:7) and that "the wages of sin is death" (Rom. 6:23), but the law that defines sin and that God declared to be good cannot be the law of sin and death. Paul says God's law is "holy and just and good" (Rom. 7:12); therefore, such a law could not possibly be the "law of sin" that works in human nature (Rom. 7:5, 23) before we are united to Christ (see Rom. 7:4). Paul asks, "Is the law sin?" and then answers his own question: "Certainly not!" (Rom. 7:7). Therefore, we must conclude that whatever "the law of sin and death" may be, it is not God's law.

"The law of sin and death" is the habitual tendency to sin that works in the "members" (the will and appetites of the body) before the sinner repents and is joined to Christ. Sin enslaved our carnal, or fleshly, nature. We were freed from sin when we were united with Christ in His crucifixion (Rom. 6:3–7, 12–13). Our resistance to this law of sin and death is the ongoing battle that Paul describes:

> I find then a law, that evil is present with me, the one who wills to do good. For I delight in the law of God according to the inward man. But I see another law in my members, warring against the law of my mind, and bringing me into captivity to the law of sin which is in my members. O wretched man that I am! Who will deliver me from this body of death? I thank God—through Jesus Christ our Lord!
>
> So then, with the mind I myself serve the law of God, but with the flesh the law of sin. (Rom. 7:21–25)

The one thing in this universe that is the very opposite of God is the self. Back in the garden it was the entrance of self-will, which came into the soul as the result of the fall, that established a difference, a separation, between the soul and God. The efforts of the self to reestablish its rule must be stilled. But more to the point, as I discussed in the last chapter, the very instance of this self must be destroyed. This work can be done in us only by God, and only through our participation.[25]

Thanks to God, a way of escape has been made for us—a way of escape from sin, from death, and finally, from the carnality that had exercised lordship over us. By renouncing our own rule (repenting) and becoming united to the Lord Jesus, we come under the law of God. As Paul told the Galatians, "For I through the law [of the Spirit of life] died to the law [of sin and death] that I might live to God" (Gal. 2:19).

The law of the Spirit of life frees us from the demands of our carnal nature (the flesh), so "that the righteousness of the law might be fulfilled in us who do not walk according to the flesh but according to the Spirit" (Rom. 8:4).

Thus, for those of us in Christ, we are no longer under the jurisdiction of the law of sin and death. We have been freed from involuntary slavery to sin, but are warned to resist the slave master and not look back.

Our Work of Salvation

All right. I've repented of my old ways; I've given lordship of my life to God; I've been forgiven; therefore, I'm saved, right? So why does Paul tell us to "work out your own salvation with fear and trembling" (Phil. 2:12)? If there's nothing I can do to save myself from sin and death, what is there for me to work out?

The moment I entrusted my life to Jesus, my atonement was effected (Col. 1:13). My reconciliation with God was complete in Christ. I became a new creation, born of the Spirit (2 Cor. 5:17–18). However, just as the slaves in America were released to freedom and an unfamiliar life, so we have been released from spiritual slavery. We became free in an instant, but old habits and customs persist.

Working out our salvation is about the process of maturing and becoming strong in Christ. Our spirits have been made alive, but our flesh is still vulnerable to temptations, especially those appealing to or arising from its own appetites and habits.

We come into God's kingdom as children, but are expected to mature in wisdom, knowledge, and influence. We grow through learning and integrating into the culture of the kingdom—as explained by the Word of God. Those unskilled in the word of righteousness remain babies. The stronger things belong to those who are of full age, to those who have trained their senses to discern both good and evil (Heb. 5:13).

Paul's statement about working out our salvation was in the context of obedience. He was telling the Philippians to continue to obey God, not because their own works could make them more righteous, but because, through their obedience, God was working in them—training and transforming them so that He could accomplish good through them (Phil. 2:12–13). They were to continue doing what we all were created in Christ Jesus to do—those good works that God has prepared beforehand for us (Eph. 2:10). In that submitted life, we walk worthy of the Lord, we are fruitful in every good work, and we steadily increase in the knowledge of God (Col. 1:10).

Our work of salvation is putting to death the desires of the flesh—our self-serving temptations. The enemy is still active. He still looks for inroads, still looks to deceive, and still leads people astray. "Therefore we must give the more earnest heed to the things we have heard, lest we drift away" (Heb. 2:1). The only safe place, the only place with life and strength and grace, is in Christ.

Peter, in his epistle, tells us that God, out of His glory and virtue, has given us all we need for life and godliness so that as we nurture those qualities and practices, we can be part of that same divine nature. He also promises that if those virtues grow in us, we'll never be unfruitful, and if we're faithful in doing the things he lists, we'll never fall. However, if we neglect those things, we can regress and become as blind as we were before we knew God. The whole passage of 2 Peter 1:2–11, where he lists this in detail, is worth reading carefully.

No Turning Back

Paul wrote to the Ephesians and told them how they should live. He also warned them of the danger of returning to living like the people around them who didn't know God. He urged them to change their ways, determine to live as the new creatures they were, and continue rejecting their old lusts (Eph. 4:17–24).

Returning to our old behaviors brings back blindness and hardness. We may say we want to behold God, but we can only behold Him to the degree that we love and obey Him.

These warnings are sobering because they warn of the consequences of not being attentive to our connection with God. However, that fear is not part of the freedom to which we're called. We are to concentrate on the freedom for which Christ made us free and not paralyze ourselves worrying about the ways our minds can be entangled again into bondage (Gal. 5:1). We are to be vigilant, but not worried (1 Peter 5:8).

It's like getting a new car with all its potential for freedom and productivity, but if we're over-concentrating on potential crashes and breakdowns, we'll never drive. Enjoy your freedom, but don't lose track of where you're going. Keep your eyes on the road at all times, and don't ever turn back.

We are called to always live in the simplicity of the gospel and to live in His presence. We are called to the ministry of reconciliation—to woo a deceived and aggrieved humanity back to a loving God.

> Therefore, if anyone is in Christ, he is a new creation; old things have passed away; behold, all things have become new. Now all things are of God, who has reconciled us to Himself through Jesus Christ, and has given us the ministry of reconciliation, that is, that God was in Christ reconciling the world to Himself, not imputing their trespasses to them, and has committed to us the word of reconciliation. (2 Cor. 5:17–19)

How do we stay in Christ? How do we consistently choose to defer to God's will rather than our own? Certainly, it's only by God's grace that we are even in a position to ask those questions, and it's only by God's grace that we are able to do either. The Christian life is a balance of grace, faith, and action. There is always a fresh decision involved—each one a step forward into renewed consecration.

The Futility of Self-Effort

I have a personal story of my own faulty efforts to stay in Christ and overcome temptation. When I concentrated on overcoming sin, I generally had one of two strategies. In hindsight, both were in my own efforts, both were impossible, and ultimately, both were crippling.

On one hand, I tried to stifle my desires and emotions and thereby make myself immune to temptation. That was impossible because I was trying to live differently than I was made. I was deluding myself to believe that if I could control my thoughts and actions, then my heart would be tamed also.

Likewise, my other strategy was also based on controlling the externals while hoping for an internal change. If I was troubled in a certain area, I researched it, thinking that the more I knew about the roots of the sin, the better I could control my heart. Again, it was impossible. Knowledge alone could not bring freedom; it could provide only an illusion of control.

I saw God's call to sanctification and obedience as restrictive and burdensome. The more I tried, the more

I failed. As I saw the people around me seemingly doing much better than I, the more my sense of guilt and inadequacy grew. I argued with God at one point, saying, "Your yoke is *not* easy and Your burden is *not* light!" (Matt. 11:29–30). The problem was that I was trying to shoulder the wrong yoke; I was trying to pull the load on my own, and my performance-based picture was wrong.

Sanctification involves both putting sin to death and becoming free to love and obey. I was doing it backward. Resisting sin doesn't come by deadening my feelings and affections, but by awakening them to God Himself. I tried to deaden myself to avoid sin instead of filling myself with the Spirit of life and *displacing* sin. True and lasting resistance to sin doesn't come through willpower or self-improvement, but through the Spirit, who empowers believers with the knowledge and love of God (John 15:26; 16:13).

Unfortunately, it is so easy to live self-deceived and burdened. My self-nature is more than happy to engineer a sham execution and make me appear righteous, as long as it can avoid dying itself. In fact, it takes great pride in pulling off such a show! The truth is that the real solution is painful, and my self-nature is desperate to avoid it. It much prefers a self-supervised charade of selflessness over the real thing. The difference is that the charade leads to pride, while true selflessness is evidenced in humility.

This predisposition to self-deception is why triumphing over sin must always start with humility and repentance, coming to Christ with no sufficiency of our own. People who, even with the best intentions and deepest sorrow, try to overcome sin by their own determination are doomed to fail. John Owen, a seventeenth-century English theologian, said it like this:

> When a man has pursued this course for a while, and deceived himself by it, he finds over the *course* of his life that indeed his sin has *not been mortified*. It has simply taken a new form. He begins to think that he is wasting his time. He will never be able to prevail. He is only building a dam against constantly rising waters. That is when he *gives up,* despairing of any success. He yields himself to the power of sin and the formality of fighting it.
>
> This is the usual result for people who attempt to mortify sin without first obtaining an interest in Christ. It *deludes* them, *hardens* them, and *destroys* them. The most loathsome and desperate sinners in the world are those who pursued this course out of conviction, found it fruitless, and then deserted it without discovering Christ. . . . I repeat, mortification is for believers and believers only. Killing sin is the work of living men. When men are *dead,* as unbelievers are dead, sin is *alive*, and it continues to live.[26]

Freedom from the law of sin and death in my flesh comes only by willingly submitting myself, *in Christ,* to death (Rom. 12:1). Only then can I be raised with Him to new life, where the law of sin and death has no power (Rom. 8:1–11).

True Understanding

When we look at understanding spiritual principles, the difference between believers and unbelievers is not so much in the breadth of their knowledge as in how they understand and apply their knowledge. It reminds me of the gentleman I described in the introduction who was filled with simple faith. There are many unbelievers who know more and may be able to expound more about the attributes of God than many believers can, but they don't know things as they ought. They are in the same position Nicodemus was when he first met Jesus. They don't understand spiritual things or the need for salvation. Their understanding has no holy or heavenly light shining on it.

In contrast, a believer may know much less intellectually, but what he does see, he sees in the light of the Spirit of God, bathed in saving and transforming light that reveals the world and themselves through the lens of love. That understanding comes from communion with God in simplicity. It doesn't come from the endless comparing and picking through of fine points of doctrine to see who is purest or from those enamored with never-ending discussions of a God they only know from afar. Knowledge puffs up, while love edifies (1 Cor. 8:1–3).

We are to guard our minds and hearts while living in an attitude of thankfulness. We are to filter what comes into our minds and focus on the good things. Paul says to *do* those good things you've heard and received, and the God of peace will be with you (Phil. 4:6–9).

Jesus is both our enabler and our example. Everyone born of the Spirit is empowered and moved by the Spirit.

In that Spirit-enabled yielding and obedience, sinning is no longer inevitable.

> My little children, these things I write to you, so that you may not sin. And if anyone sins, we have an Advocate with the Father, Jesus Christ the righteous. And He Himself is the propitiation for our sins, and not for ours only but also for the whole world.
>
> Now by this we know that we know Him, if we keep His commandments. He who says, "I know Him," and does not keep His commandments, is a liar, and the truth is not in him. But whoever keeps His word, truly the love of God is perfected in him. By this we know that we are in Him. He who says he abides in Him ought himself also to walk just as He walked. (1 John 2:1–6)

We are to walk out our lives in the same way that Jesus walked—in total harmony with His Father. Our life is in Jesus. We guard our hearts not only to keep ourselves from falling, but to keep what comes out of our lives pure and life-giving to others (Prov. 4:23–27). We are to stand strong in the grace that is in Christ Jesus as we minister the message of the great reconciliation between God and man (2 Tim. 2:1–4). However, we can be effective only as far as we remain in Christ as emissaries of His kingdom, seeing through His eyes of love and having His heart of humility.

CHAPTER 15

Our Journey as Disciples

I am the vine, you are *the branches. He who*
abides in Me, and I in him, bears much fruit;
for without Me you can do nothing. . . . By this
My Father is glorified, that you bear much fruit;
so you will be My disciples.
John 15:5, 8

KEY: Discipleship is an ongoing commitment to walk faithfully in the light, trusting God for our direction, empowerment, and results.

God came to us in the incarnation of Jesus. In His life, death, and resurrection, He showed us His Father. During His life on earth, Jesus showed us the true nature of God as He walked in intimacy with His Father and with the Holy Spirit. In His ascension, He fulfilled in truth what Adam and Eve had only grasped at. No man ever has to covet divinity again, for Jesus divinized our humanity in His flesh.

I've talked about our need to change kingdoms—from the kingdom of self to the kingdom of God. The truth is that God's kingdom is already here and Jesus is already king. It is our choice whether to stay in our darkness, where there is weeping and gnashing of teeth, or to follow Jesus when He says, "Come to Me in My kingdom of light, and I will give you rest" (Col. 1:12–13; Acts 26:16–18; Matt. 11:28; 1 Peter 2:9).

Unfortunately, and much to our natural frustration, we look for God's kingdom the wrong way. Despite knowing better, we try to build a kingdom we can see. We want to know what we need to do to advance this kingdom. But God says, "My thoughts are not your thoughts, nor are your ways My ways" (Is. 55:8).

The kingdom is wherever Jesus reigns. Jesus said, "The kingdom of God does not come with observation. . . . The kingdom of God is within you" (Luke 17:20–21). The kingdom is the life of God—the Father, the Son, and the Holy Spirit—coming to expression first in us, then through us (John 14:23; 1 John 2:4-6). The invisible becomes visible.

We must start to see things afresh. We must learn to think differently in the light than we did in the darkness. Paul tells us to be transformed through the renewing of our minds (Rom. 12:2). The message of Jesus is: Take sides with Me against the way you see My Father. Take sides with Me against the way you see yourself. Let Me tell you who you are. Take sides with Me against how you see others, especially your enemies, because that's not how I see them. Let Me take the scales off your eyes so you can see clearly, as you were meant to see (Acts 9:17-18).

The journey of discipleship is like the cave story I described in chapter 13. Discipleship is a trip into a kingdom that, in our darkness, we can't imagine. Jesus says to us, "Follow Me." All we can respond is, "Take my hand."

If you want to see with fresh eyes, focus on Jesus. See who He is, where He is, and who He's with, and you'll see the kingdom all around you. In it, there is no separation between sacred and secular.

Is this another call to religion? Only in its purest sense. Religion at its best is that which binds us to the practice of righteousness in devotion to God. At its backward worst, religion is what we do when we don't know where God is and we're trying to perform for His favor. Instead, we are called to follow the one who has already found us.

This realization is the heart of our true worship—the looking to Jesus as the author and finisher of our faith, of our trust (Heb. 12:2). Something marvelous happens inside when we realize that what we've believed about the goodness and love of God is completely inadequate compared to the truth. The very best we could offer Him was no better than animal dung (Phil. 3:8), but God doesn't see it as dung. He sees it as fertilizer from which to grow something beautiful in us.

Our only responsibility is to stay in Christ. We're foolish to go back and dabble with temptation and think that it will not open the way to many of the very troubles and adversities we struggle with and complain about. We bring them on ourselves. Sin still wants us in bondage. Its temptations can be seemingly innocent and subtle, and sin always gives us the illusion that we are in control.

Of course, we still struggle. Everyone on earth struggles, but true believers deal with adversities with hope and purpose. This is an equal-opportunity world. "All things come alike to all" with plenty of chances for horror, grief, and injustice for everyone (Eccl. 9:2). How we view those events and how we superintend our hearts makes the difference between victory and defeat. Life is hard; God is good. Don't confuse the two.

Temptation itself, of course, is not sin. What's the difference? "Temptation clobbers you from the outside and lures you to do its bidding. Sin makes temptation a house pet, gets it a collar and leash, and deceives you into believing it can be housebroken and civilized."[27] What we do with our private temptations reveals who owns our heart. Even more telling is how we talk about other people's sins. Our conversation quickly unmasks what is stored in our own heart (Luke 6:45).

Jesus was tempted, but He conquered because His heart was submitted to His Father (John 17:4–6). Circumstances are not an excuse. God can win the game with any hand that's dealt to us. James 1:12 says, "Blessed is the man who endures temptation; for when he has been approved [assayed, or approved after testing], he will receive the crown of life which the Lord has promised to those who love Him."

The gospel opens our eyes, removes the distortion of sin, and clears the fog of our misconceptions so that in Jesus we can properly contemplate our Savior, our Creator, and His creation. Understanding the basic scope of salvation, how God's plan of rescue, redemption, justification, and rebirth fits together, as well as understanding what we have been saved *from* and who we are now in Christ, is the foundation to everything in our Christian life.

Christianity is not about embracing a new philosophy

in blind faith. The goal of the Christian life is not to follow rules in mindless obedience. It is the living-out of a passionate love for God that is both informed by the mind and embraced by our will. The gospel is both completely rational and completely divine.

Keeping Our Eyes Fresh

Seeing the thoroughness of the plan of our salvation should be a comfort to us. We tend to overcomplicate things when we should be coming as children—trusting God and not comparing ourselves to each other.

Seeing with fresh eyes is allowing the eyes of my understanding to be opened through a true and accurate understanding of God (Eph. 1:17–21). It's seeing as He sees and valuing His truth above my preconceptions. When I believe God's view to be true, shift my interpretations of what I observe, and then change my behavior based on my new understanding, I have repented. Repentance isn't only about turning away from sin; it's also about embracing a new way of thinking about God, about myself, and about what's possible in His kingdom.

God gave Himself for us. We do not have to ask for more of Him. There is no greater love than what He has already given us. We need to keep giving Him more of us. With Paul, we pray to be renewed in the spirit of our minds (Eph. 4:23):

> That Christ may dwell in your hearts through faith; that you, being rooted and grounded in love, may be able to comprehend with all the

> saints what is the width and length and depth
> and height—to know the love of Christ which
> passes knowledge; that you may be filled with
> all the fullness of God. (Eph. 3:17–19)

Practicing the presence of God is not getting more of God; it is becoming aware of, enjoying, and resonating with the unbroken union we already have in Jesus.

We are complete only in Christ. He is our life. We can add nothing to His work. There is no need to go back to old covenant rules or rituals. They have all been fulfilled. Now God writes His laws on our hearts and in our minds (Heb. 10:16). We do not need to ask for more of God in our lives. He has already given us all we need for life and godliness, and it comes through the personal "knowledge of God and of Jesus our Lord" (2 Peter 1:2–3). We are to learn from Him what we have, and we are to act on what we know. There is no need to look for miracles or phenomena as proofs of power or truth. Instead, believe God, know Him, and comprehend the power of His resurrection. Those signs will follow those who follow Christ, not only as an endorsement of His kingdom, but as outflow from His life in us (Matt. 10:7–8; Mark 16:17–18). The signs follow; our eyes are to be fixed forward, looking at Jesus, "the author and finisher of our faith" (Heb. 12:2).

For those who want to live this life of wholeness—be at peace. You are created to be yourself, not someone else. God doesn't anoint who you want to be; He anoints who you are. Your story, your experiences, and your gifts are uniquely your own. Don't envy others; you don't know their story. Set your focus on Jesus and run the race that is set before *you* with cheerful consistency. Confidently and patiently trust "the Shepherd and Overseer of your souls" (1 Peter 2:25). Your unique place in His kingdom and the work you were created for become deeply satisfying as you grow in understanding (Eph. 2:10).

Go deeper. Investigate. Ask the hard questions—the ones you have been afraid to ask or haven't allowed yourself to ask. The more you learn about God and the more intimately you come to know God, the more wonderfully He reveals Himself to you. As the eyes of your understanding are opened, you not only see God with less distortion, but you will see yourself with fresh eyes; you will see yourself as He sees you.

In the end, just taking a quick glance at these things is easy, but it's also superficial, because it's not what you look at that matters. It's what you *see*—and seeing requires vulnerability. Take time and let His light reveal each of you; see Him as the God He is—the one who created you and has always loved you, the one who has provided for you, covered your nakedness, and removed your shame. Then, allow Him to show you yourself through His eyes—His child of destiny, intimately loved, and never forsaken. Look on Him with fresh eyes of faith, knowing God is good, and allow yourself to be caught up in the seeing of His glory, grace, and freedom. Allow yourself to both see and be seen (1 Cor. 13:12). We are destined to be like Him (1 John 3:2; Rom. 8:28–32).

Live in His Spirit and His sufficiency (Gal. 5:24–25). Take your eyes off yourself and go forth in His Spirit and in His love. Teach His truth, make disciples, and where you find darkness, advance His kingdom of light.

BECOMING A FOLLOWER OF JESUS

*Come to Me, all you who labor and are heavy
laden, and I will give you rest.
Take My yoke upon you and learn from Me, for
I am gentle and lowly in heart, and you will find
rest for your souls.*
Matthew 11:28–29

Many people spend their lives being their own savior. They pride themselves on their ability to make good choices, find ways to get out of their difficulties, and make a good life for themselves.

Jesus never came up to anyone and said, "Let Me into your heart," or "Accept Me." Instead, as He said to the fishermen in Matthew 4:19, His call is "Follow Me." Those men left their nets, left their own concerns, and followed Jesus. They left the lives they had and joined His—and began a life of understanding.

This is a book about the goodness of the salvation that God has provided for us. There is a prayer of consecration at the end, but please know this is only an example. Your choice to follow Jesus is not about the words. It's not a choice from your head—a calculated strategy to have a better life or avoid eternal disaster. Your choice to follow Jesus must be seriously considered, and it must be from your heart. At its core, the decision to make Jesus the Lord of your life is an abdication from your rule in the kingdom of self—a decision to give up your self-interests and submit to your death. "Jesus said to His disciples, 'If anyone desires to come after Me, let him deny himself, and take up his cross, and follow Me. For whoever desires to save his life will lose it, but whoever loses his life for My sake will find it'" (Matt. 16:24–25).

I trust this book has made it clear: we find His life only when we lose our own. Salvation is not an enhancement or upgrade of the life we live now. It is a replacement. It starts with repenting for a life lived in ignorance and rebellion to God. Out of that confession comes your resolution and commitment that Jesus is now your Lord and that His commands will now direct you. You entrust yourself to Him for your salvation. You are welcomed into His rest.

Jesus said that anyone who comes to Him in faith will not be rejected (John 6:37). Pray to Him from your heart. Let your words come from there. There is no script; there is only your loving Father waiting to hear your voice.

Trust His love for you, and you will find true life, true freedom, and rest for your soul.

Prayer of Consecration and Commitment

I take God the Father to be my God;
I take God the Son to be my Savior;
I take God the Holy Spirit to be my Sanctifier;
I take the Word of God to be my rule;
I take the people of God to be my people;
I do hereby dedicate and yield my whole self
to the Lord;
And I do this deliberately, freely, and forever.
Amen.[28]

DISCUSSION QUESTIONS

1. How has this book changed your concept of God and how He works in a person's life? What surprised you the most?

2. Is it important to ask questions about what you believe, or does it show a lack of faith?

3. What aspects of God's character do you tend to focus on: creator/judge or loving father? Why?

4. Looking is different than seeing. In what ways are humility and vulnerability the keys to seeing truth in a fresh way?

5. Some people say that the story of Adam and Eve in the book of Genesis isn't true at all. Others say it is true and must be read absolutely literally. Others contend that the story contains and illustrates truth and is written in such a way that the simplest person can understand the message. Wise men have argued for millennia over these questions. However, for the purpose of understanding the message that the author of Genesis wanted to tell us (how mankind became trapped by sin and death and why a savior was needed), is it important whether the story is literal or figurative if it effectively communicates the truth? Why or why not?

6. When God put the Tree of the Knowledge of Good and Evil in the garden, was it consistent with His identity as a loving father, or was it a trap? Was it possible for Adam and Eve to live contentedly in the garden forever without eating from the tree? How?

7. Discuss Adam's sin. Was there more to it than disobeying a command from God? Based on Genesis 2:17, was God's original direction to Adam a command or a warning?

8. Explain propitiation. Do you agree with the author that it went two ways—both to God and to all people? Why or why not? Why is this important?

9. What is the essence of "sin"? How does the author distinguish between sin (singular) and sins (plural)? Does this make a difference in how we deal with our sins? Does this insight change your view of the problem God was fixing when He sent Jesus?

10. Explain the difference between "Christ died for you" (Rom. 5:6) and "You died in Christ" (Gal. 2:20). Which is more important? Is God's plan for salvation personal or general?

11. What is a Christian? What makes someone a Christian? How should we live differently after changing kingdoms? Why?

12. What is the difference between "being saved" and "working out your salvation"? What difference does it make?

ABOUT THE AUTHOR

Over John Bullock's thirty-seven-year Air Force career, he and his family worshiped at a variety of churches—from fundamentalist to charismatic. Few answered the question that had troubled him for years: How, exactly, was I saved? Applying his analytical skills as a medical clinician and biomedical scientist, he set out to read the Bible with fresh eyes, letting it speak for itself, free of his presuppositions, and discovered for himself the inner workings of the gospel and the beautiful intricacy of his salvation. John, who, among his other degrees, has a master's in biblical studies, lives in Colorado Springs, Colorado, with his wife, Cheryl. Seeing with Fresh Eyes is his debut book. Contact John at johnwbullock@gmail.com.

ENDNOTES

1. For further study on Jesus as our sacral king, I recommend *Christ the King: The Messiah in the Jewish Festivals* by Shirley Lucass (Eugene: Resource Publications, 2019).

2. Although the predominant modern church interpretation identifies the serpent in this story as Satan incarnate (either by his appearing as a serpent or by possessing a serpent's body), the text in Genesis doesn't support that view. First, the serpent is clearly identified as a beast of the field, not as a new conduit of a foreign intelligence. Second, the serpent is consistently referred to as a beast throughout the Old Testament, and is further consistently identified as suffering under the specific curse that God had pronounced on it here in Genesis (Isa. 65:25; Mic. 7:17). Third, when the serpent was punished, the body shape and diet of that whole species was changed forever, which seems hardly a just sentence for a beast that was only temporarily and involuntarily possessed.

Still, the motives of the snake are never revealed. It may have been jealous of the man (and now the woman also), who had been the ones given dominion over all the earth and its inhabitants (Gen. 1:26, 28). It may have resented being rejected as a helper comparable to Adam (Gen. 2:18–20). Being clever, it may have been trying to understand the rationale behind this command on humans that seemed so unreasonable from the serpent's experience. We don't know. What and who the serpent might be has been debated for millennia, but it is not the point of the story and is beyond the scope of this book. The focus here is on its cunning, deceitfulness, and the effects of its actions on humanity.

We do know that the serpent knew the fruit was forbidden to Adam and Eve, yet deliberately led them into temptation anyway. Ultimately, the temptation was never about the fruit, but about who God was and who man was. Were Adam and Eve no more than the animals, ruled by their internal desires, or were they children of God, ruled by God's words? Eve was tempted and then ate of her own volition. The serpent never told her to eat; it only made the idea attractive by making God unattractive. Eve did not obey the serpent; she was deceived and gave in to her desire. Adam also ate, and thus sin came into the world (Rom. 5:12). Bottom line: whether the serpent was Satan or not, the outcome for mankind is the same. The focus of the story is on man's disobedience and fall, not on the identity of the serpent.

3. For insight into traditional Jewish interpretations of the garden story and for Hebrew language interpretation in this book, I acknowledge and am indebted to the work of Rabbi David Fohrman, principal educator at Aleph Beta Academy. Aleph Beta | Hoffberger Institute for Text Study, Inc., https://www.alephbeta.org.

4. Ironically, from the serpent's point of view, it was telling the truth. The serpent was a beast and only had physical life; it did not have the breath of God within itself like Adam and Eve. The serpent was correct that Adam and Eve would not die physically. Instead, they would die spiritually, something the serpent did not comprehend. Still, the serpent knew that God had commanded them not to eat, so was still deliberately leading them astray.

5. The relationship between Adam and his wife had already started changing. She shared the fruit, and then he blamed her. They both felt justified in what they had done. Originally, they had been made to complete each other in love. They had been created to be coequal partners in God's work and live with God in the garden, but the incident at the tree changed everything. Power replaced love, so she will bear her children in the sorrow of a flawed relationship. When we come to the birth of Eve's first child, we can see this clearly: "Now Adam knew Eve his wife, and she conceived and bore Cain, and said, 'I have acquired a man from the LORD'" (Gen. 4:1).

Three things stand out to me here. First, "Adam knew Eve" is a verb/direct object construction in Hebrew. In other words, Adam acted on Eve. Their relationship, originally created in love, is now described in terms of dominion. Second, Eve gives no credit to Adam and barely any to God. Her statement, "I have acquired a man from the LORD," has no hint of gratitude. The idea that the baby is a gift of life from a loving Father God is absent. Eve's declaration is a power statement. Third, she openly disparages Adam. The word used for *man* here in her announcement specifically refers to an adult man who is worthy of respect. It's not the common word for man. Thus, Eve is really saying, "Adam didn't stand up for me and protect me; even God didn't watch out for me—but now I have someone!"

6. Robert Jamieson, Andrew Robert Fausett, and David Brown, *Jamieson, Fausett, and Brown's Commentary on the Whole Bible* (Grand Rapids: Zondervan Publishing House, 1961), 20.

7. Jamieson, Fausett, Brown, *Commentary on the Whole Bible*, 20.

8. Understanding the deadly thrust of the serpent's temptation of the woman is crucial. Knowing the underlying lie

that seduced Adam and led the woman astray is key not only to understanding the fall—and thus the scope of our needed salvation—but also for understanding other passages in the Bible such as Ephesians 4 and the entire book of Jude.

9. George MacDonald, "Self-Denial" in *Unspoken Sermons, Series II* (Public Domain), http://www.online-literature.com/george-macdonald/unspoken-sermons/23/.

10. Francois du Toit, "Note on John 5:14" in *The Mirror Bible* (Kindle: Mirror Word Publishing, 2017.

11. Jamieson, Fausett, Brown, *Commentary on the Whole Bible*, 1031.

12. Spiros Zodhiates, ed., *Complete Word Study Dictionary, New Testament*, (Chattanooga: AMG Publishers, 1992).

13. Noah Webster, *An American Dictionary of the English Language* (New York: S. Converse, 1828). s.v. "wrath," http://webstersdictionary1828.com/.

14. Webster, *An American Dictionary.* s.v. "propitiation."

15. Webster, *An American Dictionary.* s.v. "expiation."

16. The arrest, trial, and handling of Jesus were all done illegally under Hebraic law. The details are beyond the scope of this book, but suffice it to say, Jesus was judged and condemned unlawfully and unrighteously, thus violating both human and divine laws. He was condemned under laws made up by men out of their own selfish desire for self-preservation—and not by the laws of God.

17. George MacDonald, "Life" in *Unspoken Sermons, Series II* (Public Domain). http://www.online-literature.com/george-macdonald/unspoken-sermons/20/.

18. John Berridge, quoted by Matt Boswell, "Hymn: The Law Demands a Weighty Debt" (Doxology and Theology, March 28, 2018), https://www.doxologyandtheology.com/blog/post/hymn-the-law-demands-a-weighty-debt.

19. John Owen, quoted in "With Loud Cries and Tears," in *Jesus, Keep Me Near the Cross: Experiencing the Passion and Power of Easter.* Nancy Guthrie, ed. (Wheaton, IL: Crossway Books, 2009), 72.

20. John Owen, *Mortification of Sin in Believers* (London: Johnstone & Hunter, 1853) 5, 29, http://www.onthewing.org/user/Owen_Mortification%20of%20Sin%20-%20Modern.pdf.

21. Anon. "Free at Last." Quoted by Martin Luther King Jr. in "I Have a Dream" (Speech, Washington, DC, August 28, 1963). Gravestone epitaph, Martin Luther King Jr., National Historical Park, Atlanta, GA.

22. See endnote number 2.

23. National Humanities Center Resource Toolbox, "We Was Free. Just Like That, We Was Free," in *The Making of African American Identity:* vol. 1, 1500–1865, 2009. http://nationalhumanitiescenter.org/pds/maai/emancipation/text7/emancipationwpa.pdf.

24. National Humanities Center Resource Toolbox, "We Was Free."

25. Jeanne Guyon, *Experiencing the Depths of Jesus Christ* (Jacksonville: SeedSowers Publishing, 1975), 126.

26. John Owen, *Mortification of Sin in Believers*, 29. http://www.onthewing.org/user/Owen_Mortification%20of%20Sin%20-%20Modern.pdf.

27. Rosaria Champagne Butterfield, "DOMA and the Rock," Desiring God, July 11, 2013, *https://www.desiringgod.org/articles/doma-and-the-rock*.

28. Anon. Quoted in "A Student's Surrender, " in *The Christian Advocate*, Jan 2, 1913, 16 https://books.google.com/books?id=Pqs6AQAAMAAJ&printsec=frontcover#v=onepage&q&f=false.

Order Information

REDEMPTION PRESS

To order additional copies of this book, please visit
www.redemption-press.com.
Also available on Amazon.com and
BarnesandNoble.com
or by calling toll-free 1-844-2REDEEM.

CPSIA information can be obtained
at www.ICGtesting.com
Printed in the USA
FSHW010102221021
85659FS